CRYPTOCURRENCY INVESTING FOR BEGINNERS

THE ULTIMATE GUIDE TO LEARN CRYPTO, MANAGE RISKS, AVOID SCAMS AND GROW YOUR PORTFOLIO WITH CONFIDENCE

PINNACLE INSIGHTS

CONTENTS

INTRODUCTION

When my brother Chris first mentioned Bitcoin to me in 2013, I couldn't help but chuckle. "Magical internet money?" I initially dismissed it with a laugh. "Seems like a classic scam." Like most people back then, I was comfortable with traditional banking and couldn't fathom how digital coins could hold any real value. Fast forward a few months, and Chris was excitedly showing me the modest gains in his portfolio while I was still earning pennies in my savings account.

However, as I followed his journey into cryptocurrency investing throughout the years, I found myself increasingly intrigued. With no prior investing experience—not even a stock market account—he had turned small, consistent investments over time into a life-changing sum—not "quit your job and buy a yacht" money, but enough to pay off his student loans and create a financial safety net that I could only dream of.

His story made me realize that crypto isn't just for tech-savvy traders or wealthy investors – it's an opportunity for anyone willing to learn. The barrier to entry wasn't technical knowledge or huge capital but simply the willingness to step outside my comfort zone. And that's what I did, starting with just $50 I would have otherwise spent on takeout that week.

Seeing his success empowered me to take the leap, learn through experience, and immerse myself in the crypto space. I've made plenty of mistakes along the way—buying at peaks, panic selling during dips, and falling for a few overhyped projects. However, each mistake taught me important lessons that no YouTube tutorial could.

Now, a few years later, with both victories and losses under my belt, I'm ready to guide newcomers on this journey—not as some self-proclaimed guru, but as someone who started exactly where you might be right now: skeptical, curious, and wondering if this opportunity is passing you by while you're still on the sidelines.

That's why I wrote this book: to help beginners like you understand the incredible potential of cryptocurrency investing and give you the tools to get started with confidence. I know firsthand how intimidating it can be to dive into this new world, with its unfamiliar jargon and complex concepts. But I promise, by the end of this book, you'll have a clear, actionable plan for investing in cryptocurrencies safely and effectively.

So, what exactly is cryptocurrency? In simple terms, it's a digital asset that uses cryptography to secure and verify transactions on a decentralized network called a blockchain. Unlike traditional currencies, cryptocurrencies aren't controlled by governments or banks. Instead, they operate on a peer-to-peer system, allowing faster, cheaper, and more secure transactions.

As someone who has been passionate about cryptocurrency for years, I've seen its transformative power in people's lives. But I've also seen the pitfalls that can trip up beginners, from scams and hacks to poor investment strategies. That's why I've poured my knowledge and experience into this book: to help you manage the complexities of the crypto world with clarity and confidence.

What sets this book apart is its beginner-friendly approach. I won't bombard you with technical terms or assume you have any prior investing experience. Instead, I'll guide you through the basics of cryptocurrency, from setting up your first wallet to understanding market trends. I'll also share proven investment strategies, security best practices, and tips for building a balanced portfolio that minimizes risk and maximizes returns.

Throughout the book, we'll tackle common misconceptions and myths about cryptocurrency, such as the idea that it's only used for illegal activities or a get-rich-quick scheme. By the end, you'll have a clear understanding of the true potential and risks of crypto investing, empowering you to make informed decisions about your financial future.

We'll cover everything you need to know to get started, including:

- The history and evolution of cryptocurrency
- How to buy, sell, and store your digital assets securely
- The key players in the crypto market and how to evaluate new coins
- Strategies for diversifying your portfolio and managing risk
- How to spot and avoid scams and fraudulent schemes
- The future of cryptocurrency and its potential impact on global finance

Whether you're looking to invest a small amount each month or are ready to dive in with a more significant sum, this book will give you the knowledge and confidence to take control of your financial future. By the end, you'll have a step-by-step plan for investing in cryptocurrencies tailored to your unique goals and risk tolerance.

As you read this book, I encourage you to take notes—jot down key insights, next steps, and any apps or resources I mention. The more actively you engage with the material, the better positioned you'll be to take action and see actual results. Think of this as your crypto investment roadmap, where your notes will serve as a guide to help you implement what you learn.

But this book isn't just about finding another way to make money. It's about giving you the knowledge and tools to take control of your financial future—especially as cryptocurrency becomes a bigger deal and continues evolving. As we explore the crypto world, I encourage you to consider your financial goals and how this growing asset class could fit into your investment strategy.

Are you ready to embark on this exciting journey? To demystify the world of cryptocurrency and unlock its incredible potential? Then, let's dive in together. By the time you finish this book, you'll be well on your way to becoming a confident, informed cryptocurrency investor. And who knows – maybe you'll be inspiring others with your success story in the future.

1
UNDERSTANDING CRYPTOCURRENCY BASICS

Ever wondered what happens when a group of people decides money should be controlled by no one and everyone at the same time? It's not science fiction—it's cryptocurrency. The year was 2009, and something revolutionary happened. A digital currency called Bitcoin was introduced to the world not by a bank or a government but by an anonymous individual or group known as Satoshi Nakamoto. Fast-forward to today, cryptocurrencies have become a massive global phenomenon. They're not just for tech geeks or financial wizards anymore. They're for people like you and me who see the potential for change, innovation, and perhaps a better way to handle money.

But their impact extends far beyond simple transactions. Cryptocurrency and blockchain technology have the potential to completely revolutionize the financial ecosystem as we know it —eliminating the need for intermediaries, creating a more inclusive global economy, and offering individuals greater control over their wealth. From decentralized finance (DeFi) to digital ownership and smart contracts, crypto is rewriting the rules of money, finance, and even governance.

But with so much hype around crypto, where do you even start? This chapter is about breaking down cryptocurrency into bite-sized, digestible pieces that make sense, even if you're starting.

WHAT IS CRYPTOCURRENCY? SIMPLIFYING THE COMPLEX

Let's make this simple. At its core, cryptocurrency is a digital or virtual form of money. Unlike the cash you carry in your wallet or the numbers in your bank account, cryptocurrencies are entirely digital. They live on the internet and use cryptographic security, which means they rely on complex codes to secure transactions and control the creation of new units. Think of it as a super-secure, digital cash you can send to anyone, anywhere, without relying on a bank or an intermediary. It's like sending an email, but you're sending funds instead of words.

Now, how does this digital magic work? Cryptocurrency operates on a peer-to-peer network, meaning it's powered by its users rather than a central authority like a bank. Transactions are recorded on a decentralized ledger called a blockchain. This Ledger is shared among all users, ensuring transparency and security. When you send or receive cryptocurrency, the transaction gets verified by network participants and then added to the blockchain. This decentralized system eliminates the need for intermediaries, making transactions faster and often cheaper.

Cryptocurrencies have some unique features that set them apart from your everyday money. One of the most talked-about is anonymity. While not entirely anonymous, cryptocurrencies offer more privacy than traditional payment methods. Instead of using your name or bank account, transactions are linked to a cryptographic address. Global accessibility is another key feature. Anyone with internet access can use cryptocurrencies, making them a powerful tool for financial inclusion. You can participate in the crypto economy in New York or a remote African village.

But why have cryptocurrencies become so popular, and what challenges do they face? Let's start with the benefits. Cryptocurrencies offer low transaction fees, especially for international transfers, which can be a game-changer for people sending money across borders. They also promise financial independence, as governments or institutions don't control them.

However, cryptocurrencies are not without challenges. The market is volatile, with prices that can soar or plummet in hours. This volatility poses risks for investors and can deter more conservative people from using cryptocurrencies as a stable store of value. Additionally, the evolving regulatory landscape and potential security vulnerabilities also present ongoing challenges for investors and the broader crypto industry.

Reflection Section: Consider Your Own Crypto Curiosity

Now that you have a grasp of cryptocurrency, please take a moment to consider why you're interested in it. Is it the technology, the innovation it represents, the potential for financial gain, or something else entirely? Reflect on what intrigues you about cryptocurrencies and how they might fit into your personal financial goals. Understanding your motivations will help you explore the crypto world more clearly and purposefully.

BLOCKCHAIN TECHNOLOGY: THE BACKBONE OF CRYPTO EXPLAINED

Imagine a massive, unalterable book shared across countless computers worldwide. That's a blockchain for you—a distributed ledger technology that powers cryptocurrencies. At the heart of this innovation is decentralization, meaning no single entity controls the Ledger. Instead, blockchain relies on a network of users to maintain and verify records. This setup eliminates the need for a central authority, like a bank, to oversee transactions. Each participant has access to the same version of the Ledger, making the system transparent and reducing the chances of fraud. With blockchain, you get trust and security that traditional systems can't match.

Now, let's break down how blockchain functions. Think of it as a digital chain of blocks, with each block containing a list of transactions. When someone initiates a transaction, it gets bundled into a block with others. Here's where the magic happens: each block is linked to the previous one, forming a chronological chain. This linking is achieved through cryptographic hashing, which converts data into a fixed-length string of characters. Any change to a block changes its hash, making tampering evident. But how do all these computers agree on which transactions are valid? This is where *consensus mechanisms* come in. These protocols ensure all participants agree on the state of the blockchain. A common method is *Proof of Work*, where computers solve complex puzzles to validate transactions. This energy-intensive but highly secure process prevents malicious actors from altering the blockchain.

Security is the hallmark of blockchain technology. Cryptographic hashing ensures data integrity, while the decentralized nature of the network minimizes attack points. Once a block is added to the chain, its data becomes immutable—no one can change it without altering all subsequent blocks, which would require the consensus of the majority. This immutability makes blockchain an ideal technology for applications where data integrity is crucial. Furthermore, since blockchain is public, anyone can verify the transactions, adding an extra layer of accountability.

Blockchain's potential extends far beyond cryptocurrencies. In supply chain management, blockchain provides transparency, allowing companies to track goods from production to delivery. This capability reduces fraud and inefficiencies and builds consumer trust. For instance, a coffee producer can trace beans from the farm to your cup, ensuring fair trade practices and quality.

Another groundbreaking application is in the realm of smart contracts. These are self-executing contracts with terms directly written into code. When predefined conditions are met, the contract automatically executes, eliminating the need for intermediaries and reducing the risk of human error. Industries like real estate and insurance are leveraging smart contracts to streamline processes and cut costs.

Blockchain continues to find new applications in various sectors. It offers secure ways to store patient records in healthcare, enhancing privacy and interoperability between medical providers. Blockchain can ensure transparency and security in voting systems, potentially increasing voter trust and participation. Even in the entertainment industry, artists use blockchain to manage digital rights and royalties, ensuring they receive fair compensation. The versatility of blockchain is evident in its growing adoption across diverse fields, each finding ways to utilize its core benefits of transparency, security, and decentralization.

As we explore these technologies, keep an open mind about where blockchain can go. It's not just for tech experts. With time and innovation, it's a tool that could reshape how we handle data and trust in the digital age. The possibilities are wide-ranging and continue to evolve, showing us that blockchain might be the key to unlocking a future where transactions are faster, cheaper, and more secure than ever before.

THE BIRTH OF BITCOIN: A HISTORICAL PERSPECTIVE

In the hidden corners of the internet, an enigmatic individual or possibly a group, going by the pseudonym Satoshi Nakamoto, was developing a groundbreaking concept. In 2008, Nakamoto published a white paper titled "Bitcoin: A Peer-to-Peer Electronic Cash System." This document laid the blueprint for a new kind of money that didn't rely on banks or governments but operated on a decentralized network. Bitcoin wasn't just a new currency; it was an idea that challenged the very foundation of traditional finance. No one knew who Nakamoto was—whether a lone genius or a group of developers—but the impact of their work was undeniable. By January 2009, the first block of the Bitcoin blockchain, known as the genesis block, was mined, and Bitcoin was born.

Initially, Bitcoin didn't generate much excitement. Many dismissed it as a nerdy experiment with no real-world value. Skeptics called it a fad that would disappear like many other tech trends. However, a small community saw potential in this digital currency. They saw it as a way to break free from the control of financial institutions and put power back in the hands of individuals. Despite this enthusiasm, Bitcoin faced numerous challenges. Regulatory concerns loomed large as governments struggled to understand and categorize this new form of money. Was it a currency, a commodity, or something else entirely? The lack of clarity made it difficult for Bitcoin to gain traction in mainstream markets.

As Bitcoin slowly gained recognition, several key events cemented its place in history. The first-ever Bitcoin transaction occurred in 2010 when a programmer named Laszlo Hanyecz famously paid 10,000 BTC for two pizzas. At the time, it seemed like a fun novelty—a way to prove that someone could use Bitcoin for actual transactions. Little did anyone know that those pizzas would go down in history as the most expensive ever, as Bitcoin's value skyrocketed in the years that followed. Another pivotal moment came with the rise and fall of Mt. Gox, one of the first and largest Bitcoin exchanges. In 2014, Mt. Gox collapsed after losing 850,000 bitcoins, highlighting the risks and vulnerabilities within the nascent crypto world. It was a wake-up call for the community and regulators, underscoring the need for better security and oversight.

Bitcoin's influence didn't stop with its own story. It paved the way for a whole new ecosystem of digital currencies. As Bitcoin gained popularity, other cryptocurrencies—known as altcoins—started to pop up, each offering their twist or improvement on the original concept. Ethereum, for example, introduced smart contracts, expanding the possibilities of blockchain technology beyond simple transactions. Thousands of altcoins exist today, each contributing to the vibrant and diverse cryptocurrency market. Bitcoin's success also caught the attention of mainstream investors and institutions. What started as a niche interest has become a significant force in global finance, with Bitcoin and other cryptocurrencies making headlines and attracting billions in investment.

The journey of Bitcoin from a little-known experiment to a global phenomenon is nothing short of remarkable. It's a testament to the power of innovation and the potential of decentralized technology to disrupt established systems. For beginners like you, understanding Bitcoin's origins offers valuable insights into the broader world of cryptocurrencies. It shows how far we've come and hints at the untapped potential that still lies ahead. As you continue exploring crypto, remember that Bitcoin was once just an idea—a spark of imagination that ignited a revolution.

ALTCOINS AND THEIR ROLE IN THE CRYPTO ECOSYSTEM

When people think of cryptocurrency, Bitcoin often comes to mind first. But beyond Bitcoin, a whole universe of alternative cryptocurrencies, known as altcoins, have carved out their own spaces in the crypto ecosystem. Altcoins are any digital currency that isn't Bitcoin. They emerged from the need to address limitations or explore new possibilities beyond what Bitcoin offers. Think of them as the younger siblings of Bitcoin, each with their unique traits and purposes. While Bitcoin laid the groundwork, altcoins have been busy innovating and expanding what cryptocurrencies can do.

Let's look at Ethereum, for example. It's one of the most popular and influential altcoins around. Ethereum didn't just stop at being a digital currency; it introduced the concept of smart contracts, which are like tiny computer programs that execute automatically when certain conditions are met. This innovation opened the door to decentralized applications, or dApps, allowing developers to create complex platforms directly on the Ethereum network.

Then there's Litecoin, a well-known altcoin that sought to improve Bitcoin by making transactions faster and cheaper. It's like Bitcoin's leaner, quicker counterpart. These altcoins, among many others, showcase the diverse capabilities and applications in the cryptocurrency market.

Altcoins play a crucial role in diversifying the crypto market. They foster innovation and competition, pushing the boundaries of what blockchain technology can achieve. Altcoins offer investors a broader array of options by providing different features and functionalities. This diversity means another might do if one coin doesn't meet your needs or expectations. Take stablecoins like Tether, for example, which maintains a one-to-one value ratio with the US dollar through cash reserves and equivalents. Each Tether token is designed to always equal one dollar, combining the price stability of fiat currency with the efficiency of blockchain transactions. Altcoins also contribute to the vibrancy of the crypto ecosystem by encouraging experimentation and collaboration among developers and entrepreneurs.

However, investing in altcoins isn't without its risks. The market can be highly volatile, with prices swinging wildly based on market sentiment, technological developments, or regulatory news. Altcoins often come under greater regulatory scrutiny than Bitcoin, partly because of their diverse functionalities and vast number. This regulatory attention can create uncertainty, impacting their value and adoption. Moreover, the rapid pace of innovation means that some altcoins may become obsolete as newer, more advanced technologies emerge. Investors must be aware of these risks and conduct thorough research before diving into the altcoin market.

For those new to cryptocurrency, it's essential to approach altcoins with a clear understanding of their potential and pitfalls. They offer an exciting world of possibilities beyond Bitcoin, but they also require careful consideration and due diligence. By exploring altcoins, you can gain a deeper appreciation for the innovation driving the crypto space and find opportunities that align with your investment goals. Whether you're interested in the technological advancements of Ethereum, the transactional speed of Litecoin, or the stability of Tether, altcoins provide a dynamic and evolving scenario for exploration.

SMART CONTRACTS AND THEIR REAL-WORLD APPLICATIONS

Smart contracts are automated agreements that run on blockchain networks, executing predetermined actions when specific conditions are met. These digital contracts eliminate the need for intermediaries by encoding terms directly into transparent, tamper-resistant code. Think of it like a vending machine: you insert a coin, select your snack, and the machine delivers without human intervention. Smart contracts offer a similar level of automation and efficiency, making them a game-changer in various industries. They eliminate the need for intermediaries like lawyers or agents, reducing time and cost. Once the contract's terms are met, it executes itself, ensuring all parties fulfill their obligations. This kind of automation is invaluable in today's fast-paced world, where time is money and efficiency is key.

The benefits of smart contracts are attracting attention across sectors. In real estate, for example, they streamline transactions by automating processes like property transfers and escrow services. Imagine buying a house without the usual paperwork hassle. The contract verifies that conditions, such as the payment and property title transfer, are met before completing the sale. Similarly, in insurance, smart contracts can automate claims processing. They instantly verify claims against policy terms and process payouts without human intervention, reducing the potential for errors and fraud. This efficiency accelerates the process and builds trust between insurers and policyholders.

Supply chain management is yet another field reaping the benefits of smart contracts. They automate processes such as inventory tracking and payments, ensuring transparency and reducing the likelihood of errors or delays. With each step recorded on a blockchain, companies can trace products from origin to destination, enhancing accountability and trust throughout the supply chain.

Despite their advantages, smart contracts face challenges and limitations. One significant concern is code vulnerability. Since they rely on code, any bugs or errors can lead to unintended outcomes affecting the whole chain of subsequent events. A poorly coded contract may be executed incorrectly, leading to financial losses or disputes. For this reason, developers must meticulously audit smart contracts to ensure their reliability and security.

Another challenge is legal recognition. While smart contracts offer a new way of enforcing agreements, traditional legal systems may not fully acknowledge them. Legal guidelines are usually very slow to follow technological advancements, and this gap can create uncertainty when disputes arise. Until regulations catch up, parties using smart contracts may still need to rely on traditional legal channels for resolution.

As you can see, the potential of smart contracts is vast, revolutionizing how we interact with agreements and transactions. However, like any innovation, it requires careful consideration and time for society to adapt and incorporate. By getting to know their pros and cons, you'll better understand how they fit into the bigger picture of digital transformation. Whether automating a real estate deal or facilitating a supply chain, smart contracts give us a peek into a future where technology makes our daily lives easier and more efficient. It's an exciting time to dive into these possibilities, and the more you learn, the clearer it becomes how these digital tools could reshape the world around us.

2

GETTING STARTED WITH CRYPTOCURRENCY

Imagine ordering your usual cup of coffee in your favorite coffee shop. You pull out your phone, tap to pay, and the transaction is complete within seconds—just like any other digital payment. However, with cryptocurrency, this process could go even further. Instead of relying on banks or payment processors, transactions could happen directly between you and the business, reducing fees, enhancing security, and making borderless payments. As crypto adoption grows, seamless and decentralized transactions could become as common as tapping your phone today.

But before you can start spending Bitcoin on your morning caffeine fix, you must understand the backbone of crypto transactions: the *digital wallet*. Think of it as your virtual wallet, but instead of holding crumpled dollar bills, falling coins, and loyalty cards, it securely stores your digital assets—cryptocurrencies like Bitcoin, Ethereum, and a host of others. These wallets are crucial because they store the private keys you need to access your cryptocurrency. Without them, it's like having a safety box with no key. But digital wallets do more than store; they also facilitate transactions, acting as a bridge between you and the vast world of cryptocurrency exchanges and peer-to-peer transfers.

Now, let's talk about types of wallets. You've got two main categories: *hot wallets* and *cold wallets*. Hot wallets are like your checking account: always connected to the internet, ready for quick transactions. They're convenient, especially for frequent trading or spending. Software wallets like Exodus and Electrum fall into this category. They're user-friendly and accessible across multiple devices, making them perfect for beginners. But remember, with convenience comes risk. Hot wallets are more vulnerable to hacks, so security measures are essential. Conversely, cold wallets are like your savings account, tucked away from the internet's prying eyes. They provide maximum security by keeping your crypto offline. Hardware wallets like Ledger and Trezor are popular choices here, offering a physical device to store your private keys. They require a bit of setup and purchase, but they're worth it in the long term to store considerable sums as you grow your portfolio.

Setting up your first digital wallet might seem intimidating, but it's pretty straightforward. Start by downloading a wallet app of your choice. If you're more of a hands-on learner, Exodus, with its intuitive interface, is a great starting point. Another beginner-friendly option is Trust Wallet, which supports many cryptocurrencies and provides a simple, user-friendly experience.

Once you've got the app, it's time to create a strong password. Think of it as a combination lock on a safe—make it tough to crack. You'll also need to back up your recovery phrase, a set of random words that can recover your wallet if you lose access. Please write it down, store it somewhere safe, and never share it with anyone. This phrase is your lifeline to your crypto.

Security is your best friend when it comes to digital wallets. Enable two-factor authentication whenever possible. It adds an extra layer of protection, like having a second lock on that safe. Keep your software up to date to fend off new threats. And watch out for phishing scams—those sneaky attempts to trick you into giving away your keys. Be vigilant about emails or messages asking for sensitive information. A little caution goes a long way in keeping your digital wallet secure. In Chapter 4, we will dive deeper into security issues, so follow the steps as we move along, and we'll explore the topic in more detail later.

Reflection Section: Your Crypto Wallet Checklist

- Have you downloaded a wallet app that's right for your needs?
- Is your wallet password as strong as a fortress?
- Did you back up your recovery phrase (private key) and store it safely?
- Is two-factor authentication enabled on your accounts?
- Are you regularly updating your wallet software?

This checklist will guide you as you set up your wallet, ensuring your digital assets stay safe and sound. With these steps, you're well on your way to becoming a savvy crypto user, ready to explore the exciting world of digital finance.

CHOOSING A CRYPTOCURRENCY EXCHANGE: WHAT TO CONSIDER

Before buying and selling cryptocurrencies, you need to find the right platform. That is where cryptocurrency exchanges come into play. Think of them as the bustling marketplaces for digital currencies. They're platforms where you can exchange your fiat money (like dollars or euros) for cryptocurrencies and vice versa. They also allow you to trade one cryptocurrency for another. Exchanges are crucial because they provide the infrastructure to access the crypto market, making them a key component of your crypto journey.

However, not all exchanges are created equal, so picking the right one is vital.

When evaluating exchanges, security should be at the top of your list. Look for exchanges with robust security measures, such as two-factor authentication and encryption protocols. You want an exchange with a solid reputation that's been around for a while and has a track record of protecting its users. User interface and ease of use are also important, especially if you're new to crypto. You want an intuitive and easy-to-navigate platform so you can focus on trading rather than figuring out complicated software. Trading fees and limits are another consideration. Compare the fee structures of different exchanges to find one that fits your budget. Some exchanges charge higher fees but offer more features or better liquidity, allowing you to trade larger volumes without impacting prices. Lastly, ensure the exchange supports the cryptocurrencies you're interested in. Not all exchanges offer the same coins, so check that your preferred assets are available.

Let's look at a few popular exchanges to give you a sense of what's out there. Binance is known for its wide range of altcoins, making it a great choice if you're looking to invest in lesser-known cryptocurrencies. It has a robust platform with advanced trading tools, though it may feel overwhelming for absolute beginners. Coinbase, on the other hand, is recognized for its user-friendly interface, making it an ideal starting point for newcomers. It simplifies the buying and selling, although it primarily supports major cryptocurrencies. Kraken might be your better option if you're after advanced trading features. It's equipped with sophisticated tools and offers a variety of order types, catering to more experienced traders. Each exchange has strengths, so consider what aligns best with your needs and experience level.

Regulatory compliance is another crucial factor to consider when choosing an exchange. You want to ensure the platform operates legally and adheres to regulatory standards in your region. This is where understanding KYC (Know Your Customer) processes comes in. These are legally required steps where exchanges verify your identity before allowing you to trade. It might seem like a hassle, but KYC helps prevent fraud and ensures the exchange complies with financial laws. A regulated exchange is more likely to offer protection against hacks and scams, providing an extra layer of security for your investments.

In this fast-paced world of digital currencies, picking the right exchange can set the tone for your entire crypto experience. It's about balancing security, usability, and features that suit your trading style. Whether you're eyeing Binance's extensive range, Coinbase's user-friendly design, or Kraken's advanced tools, an exchange will fit your specific needs.

HOW TO BUY YOUR FIRST CRYPTOCURRENCY: A STEP-BY-STEP GUIDE

Getting your hands on your first cryptocurrency can feel like stepping into a new world, but with the proper steps, the process is simple. First up, you need an account on a cryptocurrency exchange. Most exchanges require you to sign up with an email and set a strong password. Once your account is created, you'll go through a verification process. This usually involves uploading a photo ID or other documents to confirm your identity—think of it as a digital security check to keep everything above board. After you're verified, you can set up your preferred payment method. Many exchanges offer several options, including bank transfers, credit card payments, and sometimes PayPal. Choose the method that fits your needs best, considering factors like transaction fees and processing times.

When it comes to payment options, each has its own set of pros and cons. Bank transfers are typically cheaper in terms of transaction fees, but they can take a few days to process. They're a good choice if you're not in a rush and want to save on costs. On the other hand, credit card payments are almost instant, meaning you can immediately jump into the market. However, they tend to come with higher fees, and your bank might see these transactions as cash advances, which could mean extra charges. So before proceeding, ensure you understand the nuances of each exchange and the form of payment that best suits you to avoid unpleasant surprises on your bank statement.

Once your account is ready and your payment method is set, it's time to place your buy order. This is where you decide how much cryptocurrency you want to purchase. We suggest starting with a small amount to get a feel for the process and build confidence before making more significant investments. You can buy a set dollar amount or a specific quantity of the coin. After entering your details, double-check everything, then hit the buy button. Your order will be processed, and you'll soon see your shiny new cryptocurrency in your exchange account. But don't leave it there, especially when handling larger amounts. Exchanges, while convenient, are not the ideal place to store your crypto long-term due to security risks. Once your purchase is complete, transfer your cryptocurrency to your secure digital wallet to safeguard it from potential exchange hacks.

Avoiding common mistakes can make your crypto buying experience smoother and more rewarding. One trap new buyers often fall into is overlooking transaction fees. These can add up quickly, especially if you're making frequent transactions, so it's wise to account for them in your budget. Another mistake is buying during market peaks. It's tempting to jump on the bandwagon when prices are soaring, but this can lead to buying high and potentially selling low if the market corrects. Patience is key; monitor the market and aim to buy when prices are stable or on a dip. Some exchanges offer monthly or annual plans that allow multiple transactions for a fixed fee. This could save you a lot of money if you plan to trade frequently. Analyze the best option for your situation.

Investing in cryptocurrency can be thrilling but also a learning experience. By understanding the buying process, weighing your payment options carefully, securely storing your assets, and sidestepping common pitfalls, you'll set yourself up for success as you enter the crypto world. Remember, every buy order is a learning opportunity, bringing you one step closer to becoming an informed crypto investor.

UNDERSTANDING CRYPTOCURRENCY TRANSACTIONS

When you send Bitcoin to a friend, the process is straightforward but involves a few key steps. First, you need your friend's public wallet address, which functions like your unique bank account number. This address ensures that the transaction is directed to the correct recipient. Once you initiate the transaction, it doesn't get confirmed immediately. Instead, it enters a queue where miners or validators verify it. This is where transaction confirmations come into play. Depending on the network, your transaction might need confirmation before it succeeds. Each confirmation means your transaction has been added to a blockchain block, making each one more secure. The more confirmations, the lower the chance of double-spending, which is trying to spend the same crypto twice.

Now, let's talk about the part no one likes to think about: fees. Yes, cryptocurrency transactions come with fees, which are crucial for the system to work smoothly. For instance, when you send Bitcoin, you pay what's known as a miner fee. This fee compensates the miners who validate and add your transaction to the blockchain. The larger the fee, the faster your transaction gets processed because miners prioritize higher-paying transactions. Similarly, Ethereum has its version called gas fees. These fees cover the computational effort needed to process transactions and run smart contracts on the Ethereum network. Fees can vary widely depending on network congestion. During busy times, fees can surge, making transactions more expensive. This dynamic nature of fees is something to keep an eye on, especially if you want to minimize costs.

Given the irreversible nature of crypto transactions, accuracy is non-negotiable. Once you send crypto, there's no calling it back. That is why it's vital to double-check transaction details before you hit 'send.' Ensure the wallet address is correct—if you use one wrong character, your funds could be lost forever. It might sound dramatic, but it's true. Also, confirm the transaction amount. Sending more than intended can be an expensive mistake. Taking a few extra seconds to review everything can save a lot of headaches down the line. Remember, in crypto, you're your own bank, so diligence is key.

You can use tools like blockchain explorers to keep track of your transactions. These are search engines for the blockchain, letting you check the status of your transaction. Etherscan, for example, is popular for Ethereum. Just enter your transaction ID, and you'll see details like how many confirmations it has and whether it's complete. These tools are helpful for real-time updates and can provide peace of mind, knowing exactly where your transaction stands. They're also valuable for transparency, letting you see the entire history of a particular wallet address.

With a grasp of the basics of crypto transactions, you become a more informed user and increase your confidence in managing your digital assets. Now, with a better understanding of public addresses, transaction confirmations, and the role of fees, you're prepared to explore the world of crypto without unnecessary stress.

NAVIGATING CRYPTOCURRENCY APPS AND TOOLS

In the ever-evolving world of cryptocurrencies, having the right tools at your fingertips can make all the difference. Think of apps as personal assistants, helping you easily manage, track, and analyze your investments. Let's start with portfolio trackers like Blockfolio. These are fantastic for keeping an eye on your assets all in one place. A good tracker will let you see your entire portfolio at a glance, update you with real-time prices, and even offer insights into market trends. It's like having a financial advisor in your pocket, minus the hefty fees. You can set up price alerts, ensuring you never miss a buying or selling opportunity when the market fluctuates.

Mobile apps from exchanges are another must-have in your crypto toolkit. Take the Binance app, for example. It lets you trade on the go, providing a full suite of features on your phone. Whether buying, selling, or just keeping tabs on the market, it's all at your fingertips. Coinbase's app is excellent for beginners with its intuitive design and strong security settings. You can check your balance, make transactions, and even set up recurring buys to automate your investment strategy. It's all about convenience and the ability to act quickly, no matter where you are.

For those interested in diving deeper into market analysis, tools like TradingView are invaluable. They enable you to efficiently perform technical analysis, offering a range of charting tools and indicators that help you understand market movements. Even if you're not a seasoned trader, getting familiar with these tools can provide valuable insights and improve your trading decisions. Meanwhile, CoinMarketCap is a go-to resource for market data, providing information on coin rankings, market caps, and trading volumes. It's like having a crypto news platform, helping you make informed decisions based on solid data rather than guesswork.

Staying updated in the fast-paced crypto market is crucial, and apps can also play a key role here. Subscribing to crypto news alerts from reputable sources ensures you're always in the loop about market changes, new developments, and regulatory updates. Many apps offer this feature, delivering news straight to your phone so you can stay informed without having to search for updates manually. Additionally, joining app communities or forums can provide support and insights from fellow traders. These communities are often full of experienced individuals willing to share tips and advice, making them a valuable resource for beginners looking to learn more.

Having these tools not only helps manage your investments but also empowers you with knowledge and confidence. Understanding the crypto world becomes less daunting when you have the right resources. Armed with apps and tools customized to your needs, you'll be better equipped to make savvy investment decisions and stay ahead. Understanding and participating in the crypto market becomes increasingly intuitive as you get comfortable with these digital companions. Embrace the technology, and let it work for you as you explore the vast possibilities of cryptocurrency.

Checklist: Your Crypto App Arsenal

- Have you set up a portfolio tracker to monitor your investments?
- Are you using price alerts to catch market opportunities?
- Do you have mobile apps from exchanges for on-the-go trading?
- Have you explored tools for market analysis like TradingView?
- Are you subscribed to crypto news alerts to stay informed?

By now, you've got the basics, from setting up wallets to understanding transactions and using the right tools. The next step is to learn how to invest and manage your growing crypto portfolio strategically.

3
DEVELOPING A STRATEGIC INVESTMENT APPROACH

Deciding what strategy to adopt when investing in cryptocurrency is like choosing between two different routes on a journey. One leads through a fast-paced city, where traders make quick decisions, seizing opportunities as prices shift rapidly. The other takes a steady, scenic road, where investors patiently hold their assets, focusing on long-term growth. Both paths have their rewards and challenges, and understanding which route aligns with your goals is essential for success in the crypto space. These paths represent the two primary strategies in cryptocurrency investing: short-term and long-term approaches. Each has its appeal and challenges, and choosing the right path is key to your success in the crypto world.

Let's start with the basics: what exactly do we mean by short-term and long-term investment strategies? Short-term strategies, like day trading, are all about making quick moves to capitalize on the frequent ups and downs in the market. You enter and exit trades within the same day or over a few days, aiming to profit from small price changes. It's like a thrilling roller coaster ride where every market movement could mean a win or a loss. Long-term strategies, on the other hand, focus on buying and holding cryptocurrencies for extended periods, often years, with the expectation that their value will increase significantly over the long run. This approach is sometimes affectionately called "HODLing," a term from a famous misspelling in the crypto community that has come to symbolize long-term commitment to holding assets despite market volatility.

Now, let's weigh the pros and cons. Short-term trading can be exciting and offers the potential for quick returns. It's perfect for those who thrive in fast-paced environments and have the time and expertise to monitor the market closely. However, it comes with high risks. The crypto market is notoriously volatile, and prices can change rapidly, leading to potential losses if you're not careful. It requires a good grasp of technical analysis and the ability to make swift decisions.

While often less thrilling, long-term investing offers the potential for significant returns with a more hands-off approach. Holding onto your assets, you can ride out the market's ups and downs, potentially benefiting from overall growth. But it also means having the patience to withstand long periods of price stagnation or decline without panicking.

Choosing the right strategy depends on several personal factors. Start by assessing your risk tolerance—how much uncertainty can you handle? Short-term trading might be for you if you're comfortable with high stakes and can stomach the stress of rapid market swings. If you're more risk-averse and prefer a calmer investing experience, long-term holding could be your path. Consider your financial goals, too. Are you looking for quick profits, or is your aim to build wealth over time? Risk assessment tools can help gauge your comfort level with different strategies. Aligning your plan with your financial objectives ensures that your investment approach matches your circumstances and aspirations.

REAL-LIFE SUCCESS STORIES

Let's look at real-world examples. Andrew, for example, entered the crypto market in its early days. He bought Bitcoin when it was just gaining traction and decided to hold onto it for the long haul. Over time, despite market fluctuations, his patience paid off as Bitcoin's value soared. On the flip side, there's Caroline, a skilled day trader who thrives on short-term market movements. She has the time to dedicate to her investments and loves the excitement of being connected with the latest news and analysis of the market daily. She focuses on altcoins, taking advantage of their price volatility to make quick, profitable trades. Her success lies in her ability to analyze trends quickly and execute trades with precision. These stories illustrate that both strategies can be successful when aligned with an investor's skills and goals.

Navigating the crypto market requires a strategic approach tailored to your unique financial situation. Understanding the differences between short-term and long-term strategies, assessing your risk tolerance, and aligning your plan with your financial goals are crucial steps. By considering these factors, you can choose a path that suits your personality and maximizes your potential for success in the ever-evolving world of cryptocurrency.

BUILDING A BALANCED CRYPTOCURRENCY PORTFOLIO

Diving into the crypto world can feel like setting sail into uncharted waters. The sea is calm one moment, and the next, you're caught in a whirlwind. That's why having a diversified portfolio is your lifeboat. Diversification is all about spreading your investments across different assets to reduce risk. In the volatile crypto market, this is crucial. If one coin takes a nosedive, your entire portfolio doesn't have to go down. Holding a combination of cryptocurrencies can cushion the blow when the market becomes more volatile. Think of it as not putting all your eggs in one basket—if one basket tips over, you still have the others intact.

How do you go about diversifying your crypto holdings? A good starting point is allocating percentages of your portfolio to major players like Bitcoin and Ethereum. They're the big fish in the pond, with established track records and significant market influence. But don't stop there. Exploring altcoins can add growth potential to your portfolio. These smaller coins often have higher risk but can yield impressive returns when the market is favorable. To balance things out, consider stablecoins—cryptos pegged to stable assets like the US dollar. Tether (USDT) is a popular choice, acting as a safe harbor in the stormy seas of crypto volatility. It helps mitigate risk by maintaining a consistent value, providing stability when other coins fluctuate wildly.

Altcoins, particularly those with a significant market cap and strong fundamentals, play a crucial role in the crypto market's evolution. Unlike Bitcoin, which primarily serves as a store of value, many altcoins are designed to solve specific problems, such as enhancing transaction speed, enabling smart contracts, or improving scalability and interoperability between blockchain networks. Projects like Binance Coin (BNB), Solana (SOL), and Polkadot (DOT) have gained traction due to their unique use cases and growing ecosystems. By analyzing an altcoin's real-world application, development team, and adoption rate, investors can identify promising opportunities that may lead to substantial long-term growth. Incorporating well-researched altcoins into a portfolio provides diversification and allows investors to support and benefit from groundbreaking advancements in blockchain technology.

Stablecoins also play a unique role in a crypto portfolio. They offer a way to park your money in the crypto space without exposing it to the same level of risk as other cryptocurrencies. When the market is unpredictable, stablecoins can serve as a refuge, giving you time to reassess and reallocate your investments without rushing into decisions. This stability also makes them a valuable tool for managing liquidity in your portfolio, allowing you to quickly move into or out of positions as market conditions change. By incorporating stablecoins, you can keep your portfolio grounded, even when the market is anything but stable.

Keeping your portfolio balanced isn't just a one-time task; it's an ongoing process. Regularly reviewing and adjusting your allocations is key to maintaining the risk levels you're comfortable with. This is where portfolio rebalancing comes into play. Periodically, you'll want to assess how each asset in your portfolio is performing. If one coin has surged in value, it might now represent a more significant portion of your portfolio than you intended. Rebalancing involves selling off some overperforming assets and reallocating funds to underrepresented ones, returning your portfolio to your original strategy. Tools like portfolio management apps can simplify this process, offering insights and automated solutions to help you keep things on track.

Reflection Section: Your Portfolio Check-In

- Have you spread your investments across a mix of cryptocurrencies?
- Have you researched altcoins with good fundamentals to add to your portfolio?
- Are stablecoins part of your portfolio for added stability?
- Remember to review and adjust your asset allocations regularly.
- Explore tools to help manage and track your portfolio.

Keeping these questions in mind can guide you as you build and maintain a balanced crypto portfolio. Remember, diversification isn't just a strategy; it's your defense against the unpredictable nature of the crypto market. As you allocate assets, consider both the potential returns and the risks, aiming for a mix that aligns with your financial goals and risk tolerance. With a well-balanced portfolio, you can navigate the crypto seas more confidently, knowing you've taken steps to protect your investments while seeking potential gains.

RISK MANAGEMENT TECHNIQUES FOR BEGINNERS

When you step into the world of cryptocurrency investing, you quickly discover that it's not all smooth sailing. This market is well known for its wild swings and unexpected turns, making risk management a top priority. One of the most common risks you'll encounter is market volatility. Prices can soar to rapid heights and then plunge just as fast, sometimes within hours. This unpredictability can be thrilling and nerve-wracking, especially if you're unprepared. Another potential pitfall is security breaches. Crypto exchanges and wallets, while generally safe, aren't immune to hacking. If you're not careful, your digital assets could be at risk. These risks highlight the importance of having a solid risk management strategy in place.

So, how do you protect yourself from these potential hazards? One effective strategy is setting stop-loss orders, a predefined price point at which you automatically sell your assets to limit losses. It's like having a safety net that catches you before things get too bad. Diversification, which we touched on earlier, is another powerful tool. By spreading your investments across different cryptocurrencies, you reduce the impact of a downturn in any single asset. This way, you're not putting all your financial eggs in one basket. It's like playing a game of chess, where a balanced lineup is key to winning the match.

Staying informed is another crucial part of managing risk in the crypto world. Being aware of the latest market trends and news can help you make informed decisions and avoid impulsive reactions. Follow reputable crypto news sources to keep up with developments.

These can range from regulatory changes to technological advancements, influencing the market. Additionally, joining investment communities can provide insights and support from fellow investors. These groups often share valuable information and can be an excellent resource for learning from others' experiences. Remember, in the fast-paced world of crypto, knowledge is power.

Several tools and resources are available to aid in your risk management efforts. Portfolio tracking apps are invaluable, offering features that help you monitor your investments and assess risks. These apps allow you to monitor market movements and adjust your strategy accordingly. Risk calculators are another handy tool that helps you evaluate potential investment decisions based on risk tolerance. They can provide a clearer picture of what you're getting into before you commit any funds. These tools, combined with a proactive approach to staying informed, can significantly enhance your ability to manage risks effectively.

Risk Management Checklist:

- Have you set stop-loss orders on your investments?
- Is your portfolio diversified across different cryptocurrencies?
- Are you staying updated with crypto news from reputable sources?
- Have you joined any investment communities for shared insights?
- Are you using tools like portfolio tracking apps and risk calculators?

This checklist can serve as a guide as you manage the risks of crypto investing. Managing these risks isn't just about avoiding losses—it's about positioning yourself to seize opportunities when they arise. With a solid risk management strategy, you can confidently explore cryptocurrency's exciting possibilities.

RECOGNIZING MARKET TRENDS AND PATTERNS

Understanding market trends is like having a weather radar for your investments. It helps you predict potential storms and sunny days in the crypto market. Basic analysis techniques that can guide your decisions are at its core. Technical analysis involves studying historical price data and trading volumes to forecast future price movements. One powerful tool is the candlestick chart, which visually represents price movements over a specific period. Each candlestick shows the opening, closing, high, and low prices, offering insights into market sentiment and potential trends. By learning to read these charts, you can identify patterns indicating whether a cryptocurrency will likely rise or fall in value.

But market trends aren't just about numbers and charts. Sentiment analysis plays a huge role in understanding how emotions drive market movements. In the crypto world, where news travels fast, sentiment can shift quickly, influencing prices dramatically and in a matter of minutes. Social media platforms like Twitter and Reddit are invaluable when gathering sentiment data. By analyzing the volume and tone of posts, you can gauge market mood and anticipate potential trends. Positive sentiment can increase prices, while adverse developments might signal a downturn. Similarly, tracking market updates helps you stay informed about events that could impact the market, such as regulatory announcements or technological breakthroughs.

Recognizing patterns in market data can significantly enhance your trading strategy. One typical pattern is the head-and-shoulders, which signals a potential reversal in trend direction. It resembles a human head with two shoulders on a price chart, indicating that the market might shift from bullish to bearish or vice versa. Another pattern to watch for is support and resistance levels. These are price points where an asset tends to stop and reverse direction. Support is the level where the price tends to stop falling, while resistance is where it stops rising. Identifying these levels can help you make informed decisions about when to buy or sell, maximizing your profit potential.

Let's look at historical examples to understand how these trends and patterns play out in real life. One of the most well-documented examples is Bitcoin's halving events, which occur roughly every four years. These events significantly impact Bitcoin's price and market dynamics, often acting as catalysts for bullish cycles.

During a halving, the reward for mining Bitcoin is cut in half, reducing the number of new coins entering circulation. This creates a supply shock, as fewer Bitcoins become available while demand remains the same or even increases. Historically, this scarcity has driven prices higher. For instance, after the 2012 and 2016 halvings, Bitcoin experienced substantial price surges in the following months, eventually reaching new all-time highs. The 2020 halving followed a similar pattern, contributing to Bitcoin's explosive growth in 2021, where it surpassed $60,000. Analysts and investors closely monitor these events, as they provide valuable insights into potential future price movements.

Similarly, Ethereum's price trends have often been influenced by significant upgrades to its network. One of the most transformative shifts was Ethereum's transition to Ethereum 2.0, culminating in "The Merge," which transitioned the network from a proof-of-work (PoW) to a proof-of-stake (PoS) consensus mechanism. This upgrade drastically reduced Ethereum's energy consumption and improved scalability, making the network more attractive to developers and investors. In the months leading up to The Merge, Ethereum saw increased buying pressure as market participants anticipated its impact. Beyond Ethereum, other cryptocurrencies also experience significant price shifts due to protocol upgrades, partnerships, or network developments. These examples demonstrate how market trends and technological advancements shape the broader crypto landscape.

At first, these analyses might seem complex, but as you start following the news with the following market reaction, you'll also be able to predict how certain news affects the overall sentiment and consequently drives prices one way or another. Regulatory announcements, institutional adoption, macroeconomic factors, and even social media trends can all influence crypto prices. For instance, a country announcing favorable crypto regulations can trigger a market rally, while news of stricter regulations or exchange crackdowns can cause sudden sell-offs. Learning to identify these correlations between news and price movements can help investors anticipate potential market shifts.

Recognizing these trends and patterns equips you to make more informed investment decisions. It allows you to develop strategies that align with market conditions—whether it's capitalizing on bullish momentum or mitigating risks during downturns. While no method can predict the market with absolute certainty, understanding these fundamental concepts gives you a valuable edge in the ever-evolving world of cryptocurrency investing. With practice and patience, you can refine your analytical skills, confidently navigating the highs and lows of the market. By staying informed and maintaining a disciplined approach, you can seize opportunities while effectively managing risks, ensuring long-term success in the crypto space.

SETTING REALISTIC INVESTMENT GOALS

Setting realistic investment goals is like drawing a map for your financial future. It's about knowing where you want to go and finding the best path. Start by defining what you would like to achieve with your cryptocurrency investments. Are you saving for a short-term purchase like a new gadget, or are you aiming for long-term financial independence? Short-term goals focus on quick gains to fund a vacation or pay off a small debt, while long-term goals revolve around building a retirement fund or securing your child's education. Clarifying these objectives helps you tailor your investment strategy to suit your needs and timeline.

Aligning your goals with your investment strategy is crucial. It's not just about picking the right coins but also about balancing risk and reward to match your aspirations. For instance, if your goal is long-term wealth growth, you might focus on stable investments with a history of steady performance. But if you're looking for short-term gains, explore more volatile assets with the potential for quick profits. This alignment ensures that your investments work towards your goals rather than against them. It's like ensuring your sails are set to catch the wind that will take you to your desired destination.

Consider using structured frameworks and tools to set and track these goals effectively. The SMART goals framework is a great place to start. It stands for Specific, Measurable, Achievable, Relevant, and Time-bound. By using this approach, you can create clear and actionable goals. For example, instead of a vague goal like "make money," you might set a SMART goal like "increase my crypto portfolio by 20% over the next year." This specificity keeps you focused and motivated.

Additionally, goal-tracking apps can be incredibly beneficial. They allow you to monitor your progress, adjust your strategy, and stay on top of your financial objectives. Apps like these turn your goals into a living plan that evolves as you do.

Staying motivated on your investment journey can be challenging, especially when the markets are volatile or when progress feels slow. One effective strategy is to conduct regular progress reviews. Regularly check in on your goals, assess how well you're doing, and make any necessary adjustments. These reviews are an opportunity to celebrate small successes, which can boost your confidence and keep you motivated. Whether hitting a milestone or sticking to your investment plan during a tough market, acknowledging these wins reinforces positive behaviors and encourages continued effort. Remember, investing is a marathon, not a sprint, and each small step forward should be seen as a victory. Mainly because you are also growing in the process, gaining knowledge and confidence as you advance.

As you set your goals, remember that they are not set in stone. Life changes, and so might your financial situation and aspirations. Be flexible and willing to adjust your goals as needed. This adaptability is key to maintaining a healthy and productive investment approach. By keeping your goals realistic and aligned with your personal circumstances, you create a foundation for success that can withstand the ups and downs of the crypto market. With clear objectives and a structured approach, you're well on your way to making informed and confident investment decisions.

As we wrap up this chapter, you've learned the importance of setting clear, realistic goals and aligning them with your investment strategy. You've also discovered how tools and frameworks can help guide your progress and keep you motivated. As you continue your journey into the world of cryptocurrency, remember that these foundational elements are just the beginning. Next, we'll explore how to secure your investments and safeguard your assets, ensuring the steps you've taken thus far are protected for the long haul.

4
SECURITY MEASURES IN CRYPTOCURRENCY INVESTING

When investing in cryptocurrency, security is a critical concern. Scammers frequently attempt to steal funds through deceptive tactics, such as phishing emails that ask for wallet details or fraudulent investment schemes promising unrealistic returns. Falling for these scams can result in significant financial losses. Being aware of common threats and implementing strong security measures is essential for protecting your investments. Understanding how to identify and avoid these risks ensures a safer experience in the cryptocurrency space.

UNDERSTANDING COMMON CRYPTOCURRENCY SCAMS

In the wild world of crypto, scams come in all shapes and sizes, often wrapped in the allure of quick riches. One notorious scam type is the Ponzi scheme, a timeless trick in which fraudsters promise high returns to investors, not through legitimate investment but by using the money from new investors to pay off the old ones. Eventually, this pyramid collapses when no new money comes in, leaving many financially devastated.

Then there are fake Initial Coin Offerings (ICOs), which take advantage of the hype around new cryptocurrencies. Scammers create counterfeit projects with flashy websites and whitepapers to lure in investors. Once they've collected enough funds, they vanish, leaving investors with worthless tokens.

Another one to watch out for is the pump and dump scheme. Here, scammers artificially inflate the price of a low-value cryptocurrency by spreading misleading information and encouraging people to buy in. As soon as the price peaks, the scammers sell off their holdings, causing the price to crash and leaving new investors with heavy losses.

Unfortunately, scams like these are common in a new and still developing market like crypto. They are designed to catch newbies still learning and trying to keep their heads above the water. Understanding how these scams can come your way will help you become more alert and avoid them.

Scams often exploit psychological triggers to reel you in, and one of the most powerful is FOMO—Fear of Missing Out. Scammers prey on the fear that you'll miss a fantastic opportunity if you don't act fast. They might use fake endorsements from celebrities or respected figures to gain your trust, making you more likely to fall for their scheme. These scammers are experts at creating a sense of urgency, telling you that the opportunity is limited or that the offer will expire soon. They want you to act without thinking, and once you hand over your money or personal information, they're gone.

Recognizing a scam's red flags can save you a lot of trouble. Be wary of promises of guaranteed returns. In the world of investing, nothing is guaranteed, and anyone who claims otherwise is likely trying to scam you. Also, watch out for pressure tactics that urge you to invest immediately. Legitimate opportunities don't require you to make hasty decisions. Always take the time to research and verify the details before committing to any investment. A little skepticism goes a long way in protecting your assets.

Real-life examples show just how devastating these scams can be. Take BitConnect, for instance. Once touted as a revolutionary crypto lending platform, BitConnect promised massive returns to investors. However, it turned out to be a classic Ponzi scheme, and when it collapsed in 2018, many investors lost their life savings. Similarly, the OneCoin scam defrauded billions from investors worldwide by posing as a legitimate cryptocurrency. In reality, OneCoin had no blockchain backing it, and its value was entirely fabricated. These cases are stark reminders of the importance of vigilance and due diligence in the crypto space.

Scam Detection Checklist

- Does the investment promise guaranteed high returns?
- Are there pressure tactics to make you invest immediately?
- Have you verified the legitimacy of the project or platform?
- Are there credible endorsements or testimonials to back the claims?

Staying alert and informed is your best defense against scams. Always research thoroughly and trust your instincts. If something feels off, it probably is. Protecting your investments requires vigilance and a healthy dose of skepticism.

SECURE YOUR INVESTMENTS: SETTING UP TWO-FACTOR AUTHENTICATION

The idea behind two-factor authentication, or 2FA, is having an extra level of security to your password. In the digital world, especially when dealing with cryptocurrencies, 2FA is like adding a second lock to your accounts. It's an extra layer of protection that helps keep your investments safe. In simple terms, 2FA means that when you log into your crypto exchange or wallet, you must provide two types of information. Typically, this includes something you know, like a password, and something you have, like a code sent to your phone. This second step makes it much harder for anyone to hack into your accounts because they can't access the second factor even if they get your password.

Setting up 2FA might sound technical, but it's a straightforward process on most platforms. Google Authenticator, for example, is a popular choice for generating 2FA codes. First, download the app on your smartphone. When you log into your crypto exchange account, go to the security settings and select 2FA. You'll see a QR code. Open Google Authenticator, scan the QR code, and it will generate a time-based code. Enter this code on the exchange to activate 2FA. Authy is another excellent app that works similarly and can be integrated with multiple exchanges. It's user-friendly and offers the benefit of cloud backups, so you don't lose access if you switch devices.

When it comes to 2FA methods, there are several options to consider. SMS-based 2FA is one method where a code is sent to your mobile phone via text. While convenient, it's not the most secure due to vulnerabilities like SIM swapping, where hackers trick your mobile provider into transferring your phone number to a new SIM card they control. App-based 2FA, like Google Authenticator or Authy, is more secure since the codes are generated on your device and don't rely on your mobile carrier. Hardware tokens like YubiKey offer a physical device that generates codes for those wanting even more security. They're highly secure but require an initial investment and setup.

It's essential to be aware of common mistakes when setting up 2FA and how to avoid them. One key tip is to store your backup codes securely. These codes are given when you set up 2FA and can be used to access your account if you lose your phone or authenticator app. Please keep them in a safe place, like a password manager or a secure physical location. Another mistake is relying solely on SMS-based 2FA. As convenient as it is, it's vulnerable to specific attacks, as mentioned above. Consider using an app-based method or a hardware token for better security.

Securing your crypto investments with 2FA is crucial in protecting your assets. Setting up may take a few minutes, but the added security is well worth the effort. You can confidently safeguard your accounts from unauthorized access by understanding the different methods and avoiding common pitfalls. Remember, in the crypto world, your security is in your hands, and taking proactive steps like enabling 2FA can make all the difference.

BEST PRACTICES FOR STORING CRYPTOCURRENCIES SAFELY

Let's say you've just invested in some cryptocurrency. It's thrilling, right? But now comes the crucial part: making sure it stays safe. Think of your digital assets like cash in a bank. Just as you wouldn't leave stacks of bills around your house, you shouldn't leave your crypto vulnerable to unauthorized access. Safe storage is key to protecting your investment. It's about making sure that only you can access your funds, keeping them safe from hackers or anyone else who might want to take them without your permission. This is where secure storage solutions come into play, acting like a digital vault for your assets.

Hardware wallets are one of the best solutions for keeping your cryptocurrencies safe. These physical devices store your private keys offline, making it nearly impossible for hackers to access your funds online. Brands like Trezor and Ledger are popular choices, each offering robust security features. Then there's the paper wallet, an old-school but effective method for long-term holding. It involves printing out your private and public keys on paper, which you store safely, far from any online threats. Unlike digital storage methods, a paper wallet is immune to cyberattacks, malware, and phishing attempts.

However, because it is a physical document, it requires careful handling to prevent loss, damage, or theft. Storing it in a secure location—such as a fireproof safe or a safe deposit box—ensures that your crypto remains accessible only to you. If your hardware wallet is lost or stops working, you can still regain access to your funds by using your private key or recovery phrase with a compatible wallet application. This means that as long as you have a secure backup of your private key, you can always retrieve your crypto, even if your hardware wallet is no longer available. Making multiple copies and placing them in separate secure locations can provide extra protection against unforeseen events like fires, floods, or accidental destruction. While hardware wallets are great for frequent use, paper wallets are ideal for those who plan to hold crypto assets for an extended period without regular access.

Setting up a hardware wallet is easier than you might think. Let's say you have a Ledger Nano S. To set it up, you should first connect it to your computer using the provided USB cable. Follow the on-screen instructions to set up a PIN, which you'll need to access the device each time. Next, the wallet will generate a recovery phrase—a series of words that act as a backup. That's your private key. Write these down and store them safely because if you lose the device, as mentioned before, this phrase is your only way to recover your funds. Once set up, you can transfer your coins from an exchange to your Ledger by selecting the appropriate app on the device and following the prompts. Trezor works similarly, offering straightforward instructions on how to secure your assets effectively.

Storing cryptocurrency on exchanges might seem convenient, but it comes with significant risks. Exchanges are prime targets for hackers, and history has shown that even the most reputable platforms can fall victim to breaches. When you keep your crypto on an exchange, you trust someone else to keep it safe. Moreover, you have limited control over your private keys, which are crucial for accessing your funds. It's like you are giving someone else the keys to your safety box so they can hold it for you. You're relying entirely on the exchange's security measures. If the exchange gets hacked or goes bankrupt, you could lose everything. That's why moving your crypto to a secure wallet is a smart move.

While exchanges are convenient for trading, they're not meant for long-term storage. They act more like a temporary holding space until you can transfer your assets to a more secure location. By taking control of your private keys and using a hardware or paper wallet, you minimize the risk of losing your investment to cyber criminals. It's like having your safe away from the chaos of the digital world. Remember, in the realm of cryptocurrency, self-custody is empowerment. Keeping your assets secure is all about staying one step ahead of potential threats, ensuring that your investment remains yours and yours alone.

RECOGNIZING AND AVOIDING PHISHING ATTACKS

Phishing, the notorious cybercrime that preys on internet users, is a particularly nasty threat in the cryptocurrency space. Imagine a crafty thief lurking in the shadows, waiting to steal your wallet keys. That's what phishing attacks aim to do: they trick you into handing over your login credentials, leaving your digital assets vulnerable to theft. In the crypto world, where security relies heavily on the secrecy of private keys, falling victim to a phishing attack can have devastating consequences. Once attackers get your credentials, they can easily access your accounts and drain your precious assets. The anonymity and irreversibility of cryptocurrency transactions make it even more challenging to recover stolen funds. Therefore, understanding and recognizing phishing tactics is crucial for anyone involved in crypto investing.

Phishing attacks come in various guises but often follow a similar playbook. The most common tactic involves sending fake emails that appear to be from trusted sources, like your cryptocurrency exchange or digital wallet provider. These emails are often meticulously crafted to look legitimate, using official logos and language to lull you into a false sense of security. They might claim an issue with your account or offer an enticing deal, urging you to click a link. Once you do, you're directed to a malicious website that mimics the real one. Here, the attackers prompt you to enter your login details, which they capture. Another tactic involves malicious websites that masquerade as legitimate services. These sites are often promoted via ads or phishing emails, and once you land on them, they harvest your confidential information.

Spotting phishing attempts requires a keen eye and a bit of skepticism. One of the most effective strategies is to verify the sender's email address. Phishers often use addresses that resemble legitimate ones but contain subtle differences, like a missing letter or an extra character. Always double-check the sender's details before clicking on any links. Another critical step is to inspect website certificates. A secure site will have a URL that starts with "https://," indicating that it uses encryption to protect your data. If you land on a site missing this crucial indicator, it's a major red flag. Additionally, be wary of emails or messages that create a sense of urgency, pressuring you to act quickly. Legitimate organizations typically don't rush you into making decisions or sharing personal information.

If a phishing attack targets you, swift action is key to mitigating damage. First, change your compromised passwords immediately to prevent further unauthorized access. Ensure that your new passwords are strong and unique, using a mix of letters, numbers, and symbols. Next, report the phishing attempt to the relevant authorities or the legitimate organization that was impersonated. Many companies have dedicated security teams to handle such incidents and can guide you on additional steps to secure your account. Consider enabling extra security measures like two-factor authentication if you haven't already done so. This adds a further hurdle for attackers, even if they manage to get your password.

Phishing is a persistent threat, but you can protect yourself against these digital con artists by staying vigilant and informed. Being cautious with your personal information and maintaining a healthy level of skepticism online are vital habits for any crypto investor. Remember, the best defense against phishing is awareness and proactivity.

THE IMPORTANCE OF REGULAR SECURITY AUDITS

Think of security audits as routine check-ups for your cryptocurrency investments. Just like regular health check-ups keep you fit, security audits help ensure your digital assets are safe and sound. These audits involve evaluating security measures currently in place, identifying weaknesses, and implementing improvements to safeguard your investments. In the fast-paced world of crypto, where new threats emerge regularly, maintaining robust security is key to protecting your assets from potential breaches.

Conducting a personal security audit doesn't require a tech expert. Start by reviewing your account settings across all platforms. Ensure your passwords are strong, unique, and regularly updated. If you're still using the same password for multiple accounts, it's time for a change. Next, update all software and apps to their latest versions. Developers often release updates to patch security vulnerabilities, making it crucial to stay current. Regularly checking for updates ensures your digital defenses are as strong as possible. Also, scrutinize the apps you have installed—delete any that are unnecessary or outdated, as they could become entry points for cyber threats.

Tools can significantly assist in performing thorough security audits. Password managers, for example, securely store your login credentials, generating strong, unique passwords for each account. This reduces the risk of breaches due to weak or reused passwords. Security-focused browser extensions can also help, offering features like blocking phishing sites and alerting you to suspicious activity. These tools act as a first line of defense, catching potential threats before they reach your accounts. By integrating these resources into your regular security routine, you enhance your ability to protect your digital assets effectively.

Staying proactive in security is more than just a smart move—it's necessary. The digital realm constantly evolves, with new threats and vulnerabilities continually appearing. Keeping yourself informed about these changes is crucial. Participating in security webinars can provide valuable insights into the latest threats and how to defend against them. These sessions often feature experts who share tips and strategies for strengthening your defenses.

Additionally, follow security experts on social media platforms. They usually share timely updates and advice, helping you avoid potential risks. By maintaining vigilance and staying informed, you position yourself to respond quickly and effectively to any security challenges that arise.

Regular security audits are about taking control of your digital safety. They're a proactive measure to protect your investments against the ever-present threat of cybercrime. By incorporating audits into your routine, you safeguard your assets and also gain peace of mind, knowing that you've taken steps to secure your financial future. Regularly assessing and improving your security measures can make a world of difference in the safety of your investments.

As we wrap up this chapter on security measures, think of these steps not as a one-time task but as an ongoing commitment to protecting your crypto investments. Up next, we'll explore how to navigate the often volatile world of crypto markets, equipping you with strategies to make informed decisions and optimize your portfolio.

5
AVOIDING PITFALLS AND OVERCOMING COMMON CHALLENGES

The world of cryptocurrency information can be overwhelming, with countless sources competing for attention. From social media feeds filled with opinions and speculation to blogs and YouTube channels offering analysis and predictions, the sheer volume of data can be challenging to process. Platforms like Twitter and Reddit are constantly buzzing with updates, with each post or tweet vying to shape market sentiment. At the same time, numerous crypto news sites claim to have the latest insights, making it challenging to distinguish valuable information from noise. This flood of content can be particularly daunting for newcomers, requiring careful discernment to navigate effectively.

So, how do you cut through the noise and find the information that truly matters? First, consider using an RSS feed, a type of web feed that allows users to automatically receive updates from multiple websites, blogs, news sources, and podcasts in one place without having to visit each site individually. This way, you can have a personalized feed that brings relevant articles to you, helping you avoid the distraction of endless scrolling.

Following reputable analysts can also be a game-changer. These folks have the expertise to break down complex topics and provide insights worth your time. Rather than getting caught up in every headline, focus on voices consistently delivering quality analysis. This approach saves you time and helps you build a solid foundation of knowledge.

Organizing your crypto data is another key step in managing information overload. Bookmarking important articles or resources allows you to quickly revisit them later without losing track in the chaos. You can also set up Google Alerts for specific topics or cryptocurrencies you're interested in. This tool sends you email notifications when new content matching your criteria is published, keeping you informed without having to search for updates yourself constantly. These techniques help streamline the flood of information into manageable bits, making it easier to focus on what truly matters to you.

Critical thinking becomes your best ally as you sift through all this information. Questioning the content you encounter and evaluating its credibility before acting on it is essential. Look for signs of bias or sensationalism, which can skew your perception of the market. Cross-referencing information from multiple sources can help paint a more accurate picture, as it reduces the impact of any one source's potential bias. This practice sharpens your analytical skills and empowers you to make more informed decisions. Remember, not every piece of information deserves your attention, and not every headline should lead to an investment move.

Reflection Section: Your Information Filter Toolkit

- Have you set up an RSS feed to streamline crypto news?
- Are you following analysts known for their reliable insights?

- Do you bookmark articles for easy access later?
- Have you set up Google Alerts for key topics?
- Are you actively practicing critical thinking when evaluating news?

This toolkit aims to help you manage the overwhelming flow of crypto information. By staying organized and critically engaged, you'll move through the market with greater confidence and ease, avoiding the pitfalls of information overload.

OVERCOMING THE FEAR OF LOSING MONEY: BUILDING CONFIDENCE

Do you know that jittery feeling in your stomach every time you are about to try something for the first time? The anxiety you get from the sense of stepping into the unknown? That's precisely how you'll feel as you start your journey with cryptocurrency investing. The fear of financial loss is real and can be paralyzing, especially when market volatility is a constant companion. This fear isn't unfounded. Cryptocurrencies are notorious for their unpredictable price swings, making even seasoned investors second-guess their moves. The thought of losing hard-earned money can loom large, impacting decision-making and leading to missed opportunities.

Building confidence in your financial decisions starts with taking small steps. Just as you wouldn't leap into the pool's deep end on your first swimming lesson, there's no need to dive headfirst into the crypto market. Begin with small investments. This approach lets you get comfortable with the process without risking more than you can afford to lose. As you watch your small investments grow (or shrink), you'll better understand how the market behaves. Over time, tracking your investment performance will help you recognize patterns and develop a sense of what works for you. This gradual exposure builds confidence and prepares you for more significant investments down the road.

Discipline is your lifeline in the volatile seas of cryptocurrency. Setting and sticking to investment rules creates a structured approach that reduces the likelihood of impulsive decisions. Determine your entry and exit points ahead of time and adhere to them, regardless of market noise. This discipline helps mitigate the fear of loss, shifting your focus from short-term fluctuations to long-term goals. Emotional trading decisions, fueled by fear or greed, often lead to regrettable outcomes. Maintaining a clear plan and resisting the urge to react impulsively increases your chances of success and decreases anxiety.

Consider the story of my friend Jake, a new investor who hesitated for years before finally taking the plunge into crypto. Initially overwhelmed by the fear of losing his savings, Jake started small, investing what he could afford to lose. Setting aside modest monthly amounts into cryptocurrency, which wouldn't impact his finances, gradually built his confidence. Jake diligently tracked performance, learning from both gains and setbacks. Over time, this cautious approach revealed the potential in his investments. Today, Jake has become a confident investor who makes informed decisions and enjoys the journey. His story demonstrates the power of starting small and building confidence gradually.

Insights from seasoned investors can also provide encouragement and perspective. Take Sarah, who recalls her early days in crypto, which were filled with uncertainty and fear. She emphasizes the importance of learning from experience and not letting fear dictate your actions. "It's easy to get caught up in the fear of losing money, but every investor faces this challenge," she explains. By setting realistic goals and maintaining a disciplined approach, Sarah overcame her fears and succeeded. Her journey reminds us that fear is a natural part of investing but doesn't have to hold us back.

Remember, everyone has faced the fear of losing money at some point. It's how you respond to that fear that makes the difference. By starting small, tracking your progress, and maintaining discipline, you can build the confidence to navigate the cryptocurrency world.

SIMPLIFYING TECHNICAL JARGON FOR BEGINNERS

Understandably, the jargon in the cryptocurrency world can be intimidating for beginners. It can be overwhelming, leaving you nodding while secretly wondering what on earth everyone is talking about. Fear not—you're not alone, and we're here to break it down.

Let's start with some common terms you might come across. Take "FOMO," for example. It stands for "Fear of Missing Out," and it's the anxiety that strikes when you see others making money and worry you're missing the boat. Then there's "HODL," which means "Hold On for Dear Life." Born from a typo, it's a rallying cry for those who believe in holding their crypto long-term, regardless of market swings.

Now, let's demystify some of these concepts with simple explanations. Imagine a blockchain as a digital ledger, like a shared Google Doc, but way more secure. Each transaction is a new entry that everyone can see, but no one can change without everyone else knowing. It's transparent and tamper-proof. Then there's mining, which isn't about picks and shovels but rather solving complex puzzles on the computer. Miners use powerful hardware to crack these codes, and when they succeed, they earn new coins as a reward. It's like a digital treasure hunt where you're rewarded for your problem-solving prowess.

To help you make sense of this new language, I've prepared a handy glossary that you can refer to whenever you encounter a term that stumps you. This glossary is alphabetically organized, making it easy to find what you need without sifting through a chaotic list. Each term comes with a simple definition and, where applicable, a pronunciation guide to help you sound like you know what you're talking about. Whether it's understanding what a "whale" is (someone who holds a large amount of cryptocurrency) or figuring out what "staking" means (locking up your coins to support a network and earn rewards), this resource has got you covered.

The world of crypto is ever-evolving, and so is its vocabulary. That's why it's crucial to keep learning and expanding your understanding. One way to do this is by joining forums where enthusiasts discuss the latest trends and technologies. These communities are often filled with knowledgeable folks eager to share insights and answer questions. Another great avenue for learning is participating in webinars. Many platforms offer sessions with experts who break down complex topics into digestible bits. These interactive sessions can be a goldmine for expanding your knowledge and staying updated on the latest developments.

Engaging with the crypto community and taking part in educational opportunities will ensure that you understand the language of crypto and feel confident using it. As you become more familiar with these terms and concepts, you'll find that the once-daunting world of cryptocurrency becomes a lot more approachable. Who knows? You might even explain blockchain to someone else at the next party.

THE ROLE OF COMMUNITY: FINDING SUPPORT AND MENTORSHIP

The power of building a community of like-minded people is relevant for all niches, hobbies, and interests. And it's no different with the cryptocurrency enthusiasts. Engaging with a crypto community is like accessing a goldmine of collective knowledge and different experiences. It offers diverse perspectives that broaden your understanding and help you make informed decisions. Within these communities, you'll find people from all walks of life, each bringing unique insights and experiences. This diversity enriches your learning and helps you see the market from angles you might not have considered. Whether you're a complete novice or a seasoned investor, there's always something new to learn from others who share the same interest in crypto.

However, finding the right community to join requires a bit of discernment. Not all communities are created equal; some can be more helpful than others. Start by evaluating the community moderators. Are they knowledgeable and active in maintaining a positive environment? Good moderators ensure that discussions remain respectful and informative, which is crucial for a supportive community. Check for active and respectful discussions where members engage constructively rather than resorting to trolling or negativity. A community fostering open and friendly communication is far more likely beneficial. Also, look for groups emphasizing learning and sharing resources, which indicate a genuine interest in helping members grow.

Regarding platforms, a few stand out as go-to places for connecting with fellow crypto enthusiasts. Reddit crypto subreddits are bustling hubs of activity where you can find threads on almost any crypto-related topic. They're perfect for asking questions, sharing news, and learning from the experiences of others. Then there's Telegram, a messaging app hosting numerous crypto groups where real-time discussions occur. It's great for staying updated on the latest trends and developments. Originally popular among gamers, Discord has also become a favorite for crypto communities. It offers organized channels for different topics, making it easy to find information and engage in discussions. These platforms provide a space to meet like-minded individuals, exchange ideas, and find mentors who can guide your crypto journey.

Networking and mentorship are invaluable in the world of crypto. Building relationships with experienced investors can open up opportunities and provide guidance that textbooks or articles can't offer. Attending virtual meetups is a fantastic way to meet people in the industry and learn from their experiences. These events often feature discussions led by experts who share their insights and strategies, offering you a chance to learn directly from those who've walked the path before you. Reaching out to experienced investors for mentorship can also be incredibly beneficial. Many seasoned investors are open to sharing their knowledge and helping newcomers find their footing. A mentor can provide personalized advice, helping you avoid common pitfalls and make more informed decisions.

Call-to-Action: Your Community Connection Plan

- Have you evaluated potential communities for supportive and knowledgeable discussions?
- Are you actively participating in platforms like Reddit, Telegram, or Discord?
- Have you attended any virtual meetups to network with other crypto enthusiasts?
- Are you considering reaching out to experienced investors for mentorship?

Connecting with the right community can be a game-changer in your crypto experience. It offers a support system that can guide you through the complexities of investing, providing encouragement and insights. By engaging with others, you'll find that the seemingly overwhelming world of crypto becomes much more approachable and exciting. As you tap into this network, you'll discover opportunities to learn, grow, and succeed in your crypto endeavors. Without a doubt, the community aspect of cryptocurrency is one of its most valuable resources, and embracing it can make all the difference in your investment journey.

MAKE A DIFFERENCE WITH YOUR REVIEW

YOUR WORDS CAN HELP SOMEONE START THEIR CRYPTO JOURNEY

"A candle loses nothing by lighting another candle."

— JAMES KELLER

When I first started learning about cryptocurrency, I had a million questions and no idea where to begin. Maybe you felt the same way before reading this book. But now, you're armed with knowledge, confidence, and a clearer path forward.

Would you take a moment to help someone just like you—curious about crypto but unsure where to start?

My mission is to make cryptocurrency investing simple and approachable for beginners. But to reach more people, I need your help.

Most readers pick their next book based on reviews. That means your honest review could be the reason someone else takes their first step into crypto with confidence.

It costs nothing and takes less than a minute, but it could change someone's life. Your review could help...

✓ One more small business owner grow their dream.

✓ One more entrepreneur take control of their future.

✓ One more beginner avoid costly mistakes.

✓ One more family build financial security.

f this book has helped you, I'd be so grateful if you shared your thoughts. Simply scan the QR code below or click this link to leave a review:

Thank you for paying it forward—you're making a real difference!

With gratitude,
Pinnacle Insights

6

MARKET TRENDS AND ANALYSIS

Cryptocurrency markets are constantly changing, heavily driven by shifts in investor sentiment and the relentless flow of market news. This dynamic environment sees prices oscillating dramatically, with some cryptocurrencies experiencing double-digit percentage swings within hours. Understanding the myriad factors that drive these fluctuations is crucial. Unlike traditional financial markets, crypto operates 24/7, meaning that global events, regulatory decisions, and technological advancements can impact prices at any given moment. The decentralized nature of these assets also means that speculation plays a significant role in shaping trends, often leading to rapid booms and corrections.

This chapter dives deep into the mechanics of bull and bear markets, understanding how they shape investor psychology and behavior. Additionally, we will explore practical strategies for maneuvering through these volatile conditions, arming you with the knowledge needed to master the crypto markets more adequately.

UNDERSTANDING BULL AND BEAR MARKETS IN CRYPTO

First, let's get to grips with what we mean by "bull" and "bear" markets. Imagine a bull charging forward with its horns thrusting upward—that's your bull market. Prices rise, investor confidence is high, and there's a lot of optimism about future gains. Everyone's excited, and you hear stories of people making big profits. Investors, often called "bulls," expect prices to keep climbing, and their buying activity helps drive this upward momentum. On the flip side, picture a bear swiping downward with its paws—that's the essence of a bear market. Prices fall, supply exceeds demand, and confidence takes a nosedive. In these times, "bears" expect the market to continue its downward trend, often leading to selling pressure. It's when everyone seems to be holding their breath, waiting for the next big move.

The psychological impact of these markets is profound. The fear of missing out (FOMO) kicks in during a bull market. You might feel an overwhelming urge to jump on the bandwagon, driven by the sight of others making money. This can push prices even higher, creating a cycle of optimism and greed. Conversely, bear markets can induce panic and fear. As prices drop, you might worry about losing your investment, leading to hasty decisions to sell at a loss. These cycles of fear and greed are natural, but recognizing them is key to maintaining a level head. Market sentiment indicators, such as the Fear & Greed Index, can provide insights into the prevailing mood, helping you gauge whether the market is overly optimistic or pessimistic.

Historical examples offer valuable lessons on these market dynamics. Take Bitcoin's 2017 bull run, for instance. Prices soared to record highs, fueled by heightened interest and widespread media coverage. Many investors, driven by excitement, bought in at peak prices, only to face the harsh reality of the subsequent bear market known as the "crypto winter" in 2018. During this period, prices plummeted, wiping out significant value and leaving many questioning their involvement in crypto. These cycles remind us that what goes up often comes down, and understanding this ebb and flow is essential for exploring the crypto market.

So, how do you steer through these unpredictable conditions? In bear markets, consider holding and accumulating. When prices are low, buying assets at a discount might be an opportunity to prepare for the eventual upswing. It's like buying winter clothes in summer—you're ready when the cold hits. This strategy requires patience and a belief in the long-term value of your investments. In bull markets, the temptation is to ride the wave indefinitely, but taking profits can be wise. By selling part of your holdings during peak times, you lock in gains and reduce risk. It doesn't mean exiting the market entirely but balancing your portfolio to reflect current conditions.

Reflection Section: Navigating Bull and Bear Markets

- Self-Check Questions:
  - How do you typically react to market highs and lows?
  - Do you have a plan for both bull and bear scenarios?
- Action Steps:
  - Identify a strategy for accumulating during downturns.
  - Set profit-taking targets for future bull markets.
- Considerations:
  - Monitor sentiment indicators to gauge market mood.
  - Stay informed about historical trends to anticipate future shifts.

Understanding these market trends and your reactions can help you make more strategic decisions, reduce emotional trading, and optimize your long-term crypto journey.

ANALYZING MARKET DATA: TOOLS AND TECHNIQUES

The crypto market is full of data and noise. To make sense of it all, you need the right tools. First up is CoinMarketCap, a staple for any crypto enthusiast. It gives you a snapshot of the market, showing market capitalization, trading volume, and price changes for thousands of cryptocurrencies. It's like a bird's-eye view of the entire crypto landscape, helping you spot trends and track the market's overall health. Then there's Glassnode, a tool that offers on-chain metrics. It digs deeper into the blockchain to provide insights like transaction volume and active addresses, giving you a clearer picture of network activity. It's the kind of data that lets you peek under the hood and see how cryptocurrencies are being used.

Technical analysis is another crucial aspect of understanding market movements. Picture it as the study of charts and patterns to forecast future price actions. Among the basic techniques are support and resistance levels. Imagine these as invisible barriers where prices tend to stop and reverse. Support is like the market's safety net, where prices find a floor, while resistance acts as a ceiling that prices struggle to break through. Moving averages, on the other hand, smooth out price data by creating an average price that is constantly updated. They help you identify trends over different time frames, signaling when to buy or sell. These techniques aren't about predicting the future but provide a framework to make more informed decisions.

While technical analysis focuses on past price movements, fundamental analysis looks at the underlying factors that might influence a cryptocurrency's value. It's like getting to know the story behind the coin. Start by evaluating project whitepapers outlining a cryptocurrency's purpose and technology. Think of it as the coin's mission statement. Does it solve a real-world problem? Is the technology innovative? What are the perspectives of this innovation being a widespread solution worldwide in 5 or 10 years? These questions are crucial in assessing its potential. Also, consider the team behind the project. Active developer activity and strong partnerships can be indicators of a coin's long-term viability. A vibrant community and a clear roadmap are also positive signs. This analysis helps you sift through the noise and focus on projects with genuine promise.

To see these analyses in action, consider traders who successfully use technical analysis to time their trades. They spot patterns like head-and-shoulders or flag formations, capitalizing on these signals for profitable trades. On the fundamental side, look at Ethereum. Early investors who examined its whitepaper and recognized the potential of smart contracts had a big win. They saw the promise of a platform that could run decentralized applications and transform industries, leading to substantial gains as Ethereum grew in popularity. These examples highlight how a mix of analysis techniques can guide you toward smarter investment decisions.

By combining these tools and techniques, you're not just reacting to market changes but anticipating them. It's about reading the market's language, understanding its rhythms, and using this knowledge to your advantage. Whether you're a chart wizard or a fundamentals guru, having a toolkit that includes technical and fundamental analysis enhances your ability to manage the crypto market confidently.

THE IMPACT OF GLOBAL EVENTS ON CRYPTOCURRENCY PRICES

Cryptocurrency markets don't exist in a vacuum; they're deeply intertwined with global events. When it hits the news, a major regulatory announcement can send ripples through the crypto world. For instance, when a country like China decides to crack down on cryptocurrency exchanges, it can lead to a sharp price decline. Investors panic, fearing further restrictions and market uncertainty. On the flip side, when a country adopts a positive stance, as El Salvador did by making Bitcoin legal tender, it can boost investor confidence and drive prices up. Such events highlight how regulatory conditions profoundly influence market sentiment, shaping investors' perceptions of cryptocurrencies' stability and future potential.

International political conflicts and diplomatic tensions can significantly influence cryptocurrency volatility. When political unrest or international conflicts arise, traditional markets often experience volatility. During these times, some investors turn to cryptocurrencies as a hedge against uncertainty, driving demand and prices upward. However, the uncertainty can also lead to heightened market volatility as investors weigh the risks and potential rewards. Technological advancements, too, can't be overlooked. Breakthroughs in blockchain technology or the release of a highly anticipated update can generate excitement and optimism, often leading to increased buying activity. Conversely, technological setbacks or security breaches can diminish trust, causing prices to collapse.

Historical events provide insights through which we can better understand these dynamics. Take China's repeated announcements banning or restricting cryptocurrency activities. Each announcement has led to significant market sell-offs as investors scrambled to reassess their positions amid uncertainty. Yet, these events have spurred innovation elsewhere as miners and companies seek friendlier jurisdictions. Similarly, El Salvador's adoption of Bitcoin as a legal tender marked a pivotal moment, demonstrating government-level acceptance and sparking a rally in Bitcoin's price as other countries observed the experiment unfold. These examples underscore the power of global events to reshape the narrative around cryptocurrencies, influencing both short-term price movements and long-term adoption trends.

Diversification comes as an important strategy for steering through these turbulent waters. When you spread investments across various cryptocurrencies, you mitigate the risk of any single event impacting your entire portfolio. This approach allows you to cushion potential losses in one area with gains in another. Staying informed is equally crucial. Reliable news sources provide insights into geopolitical shifts, regulatory changes, and technological advancements, helping you anticipate how these factors might impact the market. By staying closely informed about international events, you position yourself to respond proactively rather than reactively, adjusting your strategies to align with evolving circumstances.

When the world seems in flux and market reactions feel unpredictable, remember that knowledge is your ally. Understanding the mechanisms behind these price movements equips you to make informed choices, safeguarding your investments against the unpredictable impact of global events.

NAVIGATING VOLATILITY: STAYING CALM IN TURBULENT TIMES

Cryptocurrency markets are like a wild ride, full of unexpected twists and turns. Unlike traditional stock markets, which have set trading hours, crypto markets never sleep. They're open 24/7, so there's constant movement and no time to breathe. This around-the-clock trading increases volatility, driven by market immaturity and rampant speculation. Many investors are still figuring out the ropes, and speculative trades can send prices soaring or crashing almost instantly. This volatility can be both thrilling and terrifying, often catching investors off guard. But why is this the norm? Partly because cryptocurrencies are still relatively new and lack the stability that comes from years of market history and regulation. Market sentiment can shift rapidly based on news, tweets, or even rumors, making it crucial to keep a cool head when the market starts to sway.

Managing emotional reactions during these turbulent times is vital. It's easy to get swept up in the frenzy, making impulsive decisions you might regret later. Practicing mindfulness can help you stay grounded. Taking a step back to breathe, meditate, or simply pause before making a decision can provide clarity and prevent knee-jerk reactions. Stress management techniques, such as exercise or talking things through with a friend, can also keep anxiety at bay. It's important to remember that the market has its ups and downs, and not every dip is a disaster. Avoiding impulsive trading decisions is about maintaining a long-term perspective and constantly resisting the urge to react to short-term market movements. Instead of selling in a panic or buying into the hype, go back to the initial goals you set for yourself and the reasons you invested in the first place.

Using the right tools can make all the difference in managing this volatility. Volatility indices, for instance, offer insights into market mood by measuring expected price fluctuations. They act like a weather forecast for the market, giving you a heads-up on potential storms. Price alert apps are another must-have. They notify you when a cryptocurrency hits a specific price point, allowing you to react promptly without constantly monitoring the market. These tools can help you stay informed and make timely decisions, minimizing the chaos that volatility often brings. By setting up alerts, you can take some of the stress out of investing, knowing that you'll be informed of market changes as they happen.

Adopting a long-term investment approach is one of the best strategies for managing volatility. Focusing on your investments' fundamental value and growth potential allows you to weather short-term fluctuations without losing sleep. This means looking at the bigger picture and understanding that market dips are often temporary setbacks rather than failure indicators. Long-term investing discourages frequent trading, which can increase fees and amplify stress. It encourages patience and allows you to ride the highs and lows, potentially benefiting from sustained growth. This approach aligns with the idea that you're not just investing in a get-rich-quick scheme but rather a transformative technology with the potential to reshape industries.

EXPLORING THE FUTURE OF DIGITAL CURRENCIES

The world of digital currencies is on the brink of fascinating changes, with new trends emerging that could reshape the current financial landscape as we have known it for decades. One of the most talked-about developments is the rise of Central Bank Digital Currencies (CBDCs). It's like traditional money but in digital form, issued and controlled by a country's central bank. CBDCs aim to provide the benefits of digital currencies—like faster transactions and reduced costs—while maintaining the stability and trust associated with fiat money. Countries around the globe are exploring or actively developing CBDCs, which could lead to a more integrated and efficient financial system. Another exciting trend is the deeper integration of cryptocurrencies into traditional financial systems. Banks and financial institutions are beginning to offer crypto-related services, making digital currencies more accessible to everyday users. This integration might help bridge the distance between the old and new financial worlds.

Looking ahead, the cryptocurrency ecosystem is poised for significant transformation. Institutional investors are increasingly entering the space, bringing substantial capital and legitimacy that could foster wider acceptance. Their involvement could lead to more stable market conditions and attract a broader range of participants. Additionally, advancements in blockchain technology promise to enhance the scalability, security, and functionality of cryptocurrencies. Innovations like sharding and layer-two solutions are being developed to address current limitations, potentially paving the way for broader adoption and more diverse use cases. As these technologies mature, cryptocurrencies become integral to various industries, from finance to supply chain management.

Regulation will definitely be of critical importance in shaping the future of cryptocurrencies. As governments and regulatory bodies struggle with the challenges put in place by digital currencies, there's an ongoing effort to strike a balance between fostering innovation and ensuring consumer protection. Effective regulation could help address concerns around fraud, money laundering, and market manipulation, creating a more transparent and trustworthy environment for investors. However, it's a delicate balance. Overly restrictive policies might stifle growth and innovation, while too little oversight could lead to instability and misuse. As regulations evolve, they will influence how cryptocurrencies are perceived and adopted globally.

For investors, the future of digital currencies presents both opportunities and challenges. To capitalize on upcoming developments, it's crucial to identify long-term investment opportunities that align with technological advancements and regulatory trends. Staying adaptable is key. The crypto space is dynamic, and being open to technological changes can help you journey through potential shifts in the market. Proactive engagement will be essential, whether exploring new blockchain projects, understanding the implications of CBDCs, or keeping an eye on regulatory developments. As traditional financial systems and digital currencies converge, the ability to adapt and seize new opportunities could be a game-changer for investors.

As we conclude this chapter, it's clear that the future of digital currencies is bright and full of potential. With CBDCs on the horizon, increased institutional interest, and evolving regulations, the stage is set for significant growth and transformation. Investors who stay informed and adaptable will benefit from these changes and position themselves for success in this rapidly evolving space.

The next chapter will dive into the practical aspects of incorporating cryptocurrencies into daily life. It includes understanding how to make transactions, using digital wallets, and exploring the diverse applications that digital currencies offer. A world of possibilities is waiting, and it's just getting started.

7
REGULATORY AND ETHICAL CONSIDERATIONS

Before investing in cryptocurrency, it's essential to understand the regulatory structure that currently governs it. As financial markets have specific rules and compliance requirements, the crypto space operates under varying regulations that can impact how assets are bought, sold, and stored.

Countries and jurisdictions have different laws regarding taxation, reporting obligations, and restrictions on certain crypto activities. Staying informed about these regulations is not just about legal compliance—it also helps protect your investments from unexpected legal challenges, such as sudden policy changes or new restrictions that could affect your ability to trade or hold assets securely. Awareness of these factors ensures a smoother and more secure experience in the crypto market.

THE REGULATORY ENVIRONMENT: WHAT BEGINNERS NEED TO KNOW

The regulatory landscape for cryptocurrencies is as diverse as the currencies themselves. The Securities and Exchange Commission (SEC) plays a key role in the United States. They're like the gatekeepers of the financial world, ensuring everyone plays by the rules. The SEC focuses on protecting investors from fraud and maintaining fair markets. Their Office of Strategic Hub for Innovation and Financial Technology (FinHub) actively engages with the crypto sector, offering guidance and watching developments. They've been known to crack down on unregistered offerings and fraudulent schemes, ensuring the market remains trustworthy and secure. So, if you're investing in crypto, it's crucial to ensure that any tokens you buy are registered or exempt from registration with the SEC to avoid any legal hiccups down the road.

As of the writing of this book, the SEC has shifted towards a more crypto-friendly stance. The current acting Chairman has launched a crypto task force to develop a comprehensive and transparent regulatory framework for crypto assets. This represents an essential change in the crypto world and one we should watch for future developments.

Across the pond, the United Kingdom's Financial Conduct Authority (FCA) is the equivalent watchdog. They set the rules for promoting crypto assets and demand that firms be authorized or registered to market them. Before any crypto company can start advertising their shiny new coin to UK consumers, they must pass the FCA's stringent checks. It's all part of an effort to prevent misleading promotions and protect consumers from high-risk investments. The FCA's guidelines also emphasize transparency, ensuring investors understand the risks. If you're in the UK, it's wise to check whether the firm you're dealing with is FCA-authorized. This small step can save you from scams and ensure you deal with reputable companies.

Regulations don't just exist to keep companies in check; they also significantly impact the market as a whole. They can send shockwaves through the crypto markets when major regulatory announcements hit. Prices might skyrocket or plummet, depending on whether the news is positive or negative. For instance, a friendly regulatory stance can boost investor confidence, leading to increased buying, while a crackdown might cause a sell-off. However, regulations also have a stabilizing role, preventing market manipulation and protecting investors from fraud. By ensuring that market players abide by certain standards, regulators help sustain a fair and orderly market. This stability benefits long-term investors who prefer predictability over wild market swings.

One of the most enduring challenges in the regulatory space is balancing innovation with consumer protection. Cryptocurrencies are constantly evolving, with new technologies and applications emerging rapidly. Regulators must keep up with these changes while ensuring investors are not exposed to undue risks. It's a delicate dance, requiring flexible rules to accommodate innovation yet firm enough to prevent abuse. And then there's the issue of cross-border transactions. Cryptocurrencies know no borders, but regulations do. This creates jurisdictional challenges, as transactions often involve multiple countries with differing rules. Addressing these complexities is an ongoing task for regulators worldwide.

For investors, compliance is about avoiding fines and peace of mind. Understanding Know Your Customer (KYC) and Anti-Money Laundering (AML) requirements is a good starting point. These rules require investors to verify their identities, helping to prevent fraud and money laundering. KYC processes might feel like a hassle, but they're designed to protect you and maintain the market's integrity. Additionally, keeping detailed records of your transactions is crucial for tax purposes. Whether you're buying, selling, or trading crypto, having accurate records will ensure you're ready when tax season comes. This keeps you compliant with tax laws and helps you manage your investments more effectively.

ETHICAL INVESTING IN CRYPTOCURRENCY: WHAT IT MEANS

Ethical investing is more than just a trend—it's a commitment to align your investments with your values. In the world of cryptocurrency, this means looking beyond potential profits and considering the environmental, social, and governance (ESG) factors that come into play. ESG is a set of criteria used to evaluate a company's operations and ethical impact. In the crypto space, this means examining how cryptocurrencies are mined, their environmental footprint, how they contribute to society, and how transparent and accountable the projects are. It's about making sure your investments are financially rewarding and also socially and environmentally responsible.

Let's start with the environmental implications of crypto mining, a hot topic in the ethical investing community. Mining, especially with cryptocurrencies that use Proof of Work (PoW) like Bitcoin, requires immense energy, often leading to high carbon emissions. This energy consumption has sparked debates over sustainability, with critics arguing that the environmental cost outweighs the benefits. However, the industry is evolving, and many projects are shifting towards more sustainable practices. Some cryptocurrencies are transitioning to Proof of Stake (PoS) systems, which consume significantly less energy. Meanwhile, others are exploring innovative solutions like using renewable energy sources for mining operations. This shift demonstrates a growing awareness of environmental responsibility within the crypto community.

Social concerns in crypto mining primarily revolve around environmental impact, but labor-related issues can also arise in specific contexts. Large-scale mining farms, particularly in regions with weak labor protections, may expose workers, such as technicians and maintenance staff, to poor working conditions, including excessive heat, noise, and long hours. Additionally, some operations have been linked to electricity theft or unfair resource allocation, which can negatively impact local communities. Ethical investors should consider not only how cryptocurrencies are mined but also the sustainability and fairness of mining practices. Supporting projects that use renewable energy and responsibly sourced hardware can promote better industry standards while ensuring a more positive impact on workers and communities involved in the broader supply chain.

Transparency is another cornerstone of ethical investing in crypto. Investors should seek out projects that are open about their operations and governance. This often starts with thoroughly evaluating a project's whitepaper, which outlines its goals, technology, and team. A well-documented whitepaper indicates a project's commitment to transparency and accountability. Additionally, researching the team's background can provide insights into their expertise and integrity. Open-source development is another indicator of transparency, allowing the community to review and contribute to the project's code. This openness fosters trust and collaboration, which is essential for any successful crypto project.

Identifying ethical investment opportunities in the crypto world requires a discerning eye. Look for projects with clear social impact goals, such as those aimed at improving financial inclusion or supporting renewable energy initiatives. Community-driven initiatives are also worth exploring. These projects often prioritize the needs and interests of their users, promoting a sense of shared ownership and responsibility. By investing in such projects, you can align your financial goals with your ethical values, contributing to positive change while pursuing returns. This approach enhances your investment portfolio and reinforces your commitment to responsible investing.

The vast landscape of cryptocurrency can be challenging, especially when trying to adhere to ethical standards. But by focusing on environmental, social, and governance factors, you can make informed decisions that reflect your values. Whether it's supporting projects that use sustainable energy, ensuring fair labor practices in mining, or demanding transparency from crypto teams, your investment choices have the power to drive meaningful change. As the crypto industry continues to evolve, ethical investing will play a crucial role in shaping its future, offering a path that balances profitability with responsibility.

NAVIGATING TAX IMPLICATIONS OF CRYPTO INVESTMENTS

Yes, Uncle Sam wants his share, even in the digital world of crypto. When you trade cryptocurrencies, you're subject to capital gains tax. This works just like it does with stocks or real estate. If you sell your crypto for more than you paid, that's a gain. If you sell it for less, that's a loss. These gains or losses could be short-term or long-term, depending on how long you've held the asset. Short-term gains (for assets held less than a year) are usually taxed at a higher rate than long-term gains. Understanding these distinctions is important because they directly affect how much tax you owe.

But trading isn't the only thing that can trigger taxes. If you're into mining cryptocurrencies, the IRS considers any rewards you earn as taxable income. This means you need to report the fair market value of the coins at the time you receive them. Think of it like getting paid in crypto instead of dollars. This income could push you into a higher tax bracket, so plan accordingly. And if you're receiving crypto as payment for services, the same rules apply. You'll need to convert the value of that payment to dollars and report it as income. It's all part of staying on the right side of tax regulations and keeping your financial affairs in order.

Now, let's talk about record-keeping, which might not be the most glamorous part of investing but is hugely important. Keeping accurate records is not just about compliance but peace of mind. You'll need to track every transaction—from the date and value to the purpose and parties involved. This helps you calculate the cost basis of your assets, which is crucial for determining gains or losses. If you're trading frequently, consider using a crypto-specific tax software tool. These tools can automatically track your transactions and generate the necessary tax forms, saving time and reducing errors. And don't forget to document everything—even a tiny oversight can lead to big headaches.

If you're looking to minimize your tax liabilities legally, there are a few strategies you might consider. One popular approach is tax-loss harvesting which involves selling assets to realize a capital loss to offset gains elsewhere in your portfolio. It's a smart way to reduce your taxable income, especially in a volatile market where prices can swing dramatically. Another strategy is holding your crypto for over a year before selling. This way, you benefit from lower long-term capital gains rates. You can also explore using tax-efficient accounts to shield your gains from taxes further if available. But remember, these strategies require careful planning and consultation with a tax professional to ensure they're executed correctly.

Ignoring tax obligations might seem tempting, but the consequences of non-compliance are severe. Failing to report crypto transactions can lead to hefty fines and penalties. The IRS is intensifying enforcement on crypto tax evasion and has the tools to track unreported gains. Legal challenges from tax authorities can be time-consuming and expensive, not to mention the stress they bring. So, it pays to be proactive. Stay informed about the latest tax rules, and don't hesitate to seek professional advice if you're unsure how to handle your crypto taxes. Being diligent now can save you from a world of trouble later on.

UNDERSTANDING CRYPTOCURRENCY'S ROLE IN FINANCIAL INCLUSION

Financial inclusion is more than a trendy term; it's about opening doors to financial services for those left out. Imagine living where banks are scarce and accessing essential financial services is as tricky as finding clean water in a desert. That's the reality for many people across the globe. Cryptocurrencies swoop here like a game-changer, offering a fresh way to bridge the gap. At its core, financial inclusion means giving everyone, especially the unbanked, access to the financial services they need. It's about leveling the playing field and ensuring everyone can participate in the economy, regardless of where they live or how much money they have.

Cryptocurrencies can significantly enhance financial access, especially for underserved communities. They lower transaction costs, making it cheaper to send money across borders. Think of it this way: sending money home from abroad through traditional channels often comes with hefty fees that eat into the amount your family receives. Crypto remittances slash these costs, putting more money in the hands of those who need it most. Plus, digital currencies enable microtransactions and peer-to-peer lending. This means even the smallest amounts can be transferred or borrowed without the fees that typically make such transactions impractical. These small savings can lead to considerable changes for communities where every penny counts.

There are some inspiring examples of how cryptocurrencies are driving financial inclusion. Take Stellar, for instance. This platform partners with financial institutions to facilitate transactions between countries, making it easier and cheaper for people to send money home. Then there's AZA Finance (formerly BitPesa), which has significantly impacted remittances in Africa. Using Bitcoin, AZA Finance cuts the costs and time associated with traditional remittance services. Since its inception, it has shifted its focus from individual remittances to business-to-business (B2B) payments, helping companies settle cross-border transactions efficiently. These projects show that crypto isn't just about speculation or tech geeks; it's about real-world solutions that make a difference in people's lives.

Yet, despite these successes, challenges remain. Technological barriers can be a significant hurdle in developing regions with limited or unreliable internet access. Without reliable connectivity, accessing and using cryptocurrencies becomes a struggle. This lack of infrastructure is a significant roadblock, preventing many from reaping digital currencies' benefits. Additionally, regulatory hurdles often impede adoption. While crypto can operate beyond borders, it still faces local regulations that can either enable or stifle its growth. Working through these regulatory landscapes can be tricky, as countries have varying rules and attitudes towards cryptocurrencies. These challenges show the need for ongoing efforts to improve access and create favorable conditions for crypto to thrive.

Recognizing the potential of cryptocurrencies in promoting financial inclusion is crucial. They offer a way to extend financial services to those who need them most, helping to create a more equitable economic system. By addressing the challenges and working towards solutions, cryptocurrencies can become a powerful force for good, transforming the financial space and bringing everyone into the fold.

As we move forward, it's essential to continue exploring how digital currencies can be leveraged to improve financial access for all. The journey towards financial inclusion is long, but with the right tools and commitment, it's a goal that's increasingly within reach.

8
ADVANCED CONCEPTS SIMPLIFIED FOR BEGINNERS

Have you ever imagined a world where money transactions are not dependent on banks to move hands, and everything is directly controlled peer-to-peer? That's the world of Decentralized Finance, or DeFi, where traditional financial systems are reimagined using blockchain technology. DeFi is like the rebellious teenager of the financial world, determined to do things differently and cut out the middlemen. It's all about directly providing financial services—like lending, borrowing, and trading—between users without relying on banks or other intermediaries. This concept isn't just about being different for the sake of it. DeFi aims to make financial processes faster, cheaper, and more transparent, offering you more control over your financial future. By leveraging blockchain, DeFi creates a secure environment where transactions are recorded in clear, unalterable files called blocks. This setup reduces costs and transaction times and enhances security and autonomy, allowing you to take charge of your finances in ways previously reserved for big institutions.

The real magic of DeFi lies in its applications and the protocols that power them. You could, for example, get a loan without the hassle of a bank application. DeFi platforms like Aave allow you to lend or borrow digital assets directly from other users. These platforms use smart contracts, which are automated agreements where all terms and conditions are encoded directly into software. These digital contracts execute automatically when predefined conditions are met, ensuring everything runs smoothly without human intervention. Then there are decentralized exchanges, or DEXs, like Uniswap, where you can trade cryptocurrencies directly with peers. No central authority controls the trade, making the process more democratic and accessible.

Another hot topic in DeFi is yield farming, a popular DeFi strategy that enables participants to collect incentives by allocating their crypto assets to various platforms. When you provide assets to a liquidity pool, you make your cryptocurrency available for other users to trade against. Here's how it works: let's say there's a pool for trading ETH and USDC. You deposit equal values of both tokens into the pool. When other users want to swap between these tokens, they use the assets you've provided. Each trade has a small fee attached to it. As a liquidity provider, you earn a portion of these trading fees. However, it's important to note that providing liquidity carries risks since you would not have access to your assets for a period of time, leaving you vulnerable to losses in case prices change significantly.

While DeFi offers exciting new possibilities, it's not without risks. One of the biggest draws of DeFi is its increased accessibility and innovation. By removing intermediaries, DeFi opens up financial services to anyone with access to the internet, breaking down barriers that have kept many people out of the traditional financial system. However, this comes with challenges. Smart contracts, while innovative, are not foolproof. They can have vulnerabilities in their code, which hackers could exploit, leading to significant losses. And because the DeFi space is largely unregulated, there's a level of uncertainty that can make new investors nervous. This lack of regulation also means that if something goes wrong, there might not be legal recourse to recover lost funds. Despite these risks, many people find the potential rewards worth the gamble, especially with the proper precautions.

To get started with DeFi, you'll need some tools. First up is Metamask, a digital wallet that acts as your gateway to the DeFi world. You can use it to store and manage your cryptocurrencies, access DeFi platforms, and execute transactions, all from your browser. It's user-friendly, even for beginners, making it a great starting point for exploring DeFi opportunities. Once you're up and running, keeping track of your DeFi portfolio is crucial. Tools like Zapper simplify this, offering a comprehensive overview of your assets, investments, and earnings. Zapper connects to your wallet, providing insights into your DeFi activities and helping you manage your investments more effectively. These tools simplify the process and empower you to make informed decisions about your financial future.

While DeFi has captured significant attention, Web3 encompasses a much broader vision that's worth understanding as you begin your crypto journey. Imagine the internet you use today as a vast network where you're primarily a consumer—you browse websites owned by corporations, share personal information that becomes their property, and have little say in how these platforms evolve. Web3 flips this dynamic entirely on its head. It's like comparing renting an apartment where you follow someone else's rules to building your own home exactly how you want it.

As you explore the world of DeFi, remember that it's still in its infancy. The reality is constantly evolving, with new projects and innovations always emerging. Staying informed and cautious is key to navigating this space successfully. Consider starting small, experimenting with different platforms, and gradually expanding your involvement as you gain confidence. DeFi represents the arrival of a future where financial services are more inclusive, efficient, and empowering for everyone.

However, DeFi is just one piece of the larger Web3 ecosystem, which aims to decentralize finance, identity, data ownership, and online interactions. The same principles that drive DeFi—removing intermediaries, enhancing transparency, and promoting user control—are shaping the future of the internet itself. With the right tools and knowledge, you can participate in this exciting transformation and discover how decentralized finance fits into the broader vision of Web3, where individuals have more autonomy over their digital lives.

HOW MINING WORKS: SIMPLIFIED FOR BEGINNERS

Have you ever wondered how those mysterious digital coins came into existence? It's all thanks to a process called cryptocurrency mining. It's like a digital treasure hunt, where participants have to solve complex mathematical puzzles to validate transactions on the blockchain. These puzzles are like securing a digital vault; those who solve them first get rewarded with new cryptocurrency. This process is crucial because it keeps the blockchain secure and ensures all transactions are legitimate. By adding new transactions to the blockchain, miners help maintain the integrity of the entire network. Mining is the backbone that keeps cryptocurrencies decentralized and secure, functioning without a central authority overseeing everything.

There are different ways to mine, and each has its unique twist. The most well-known method is Proof of Work (PoW), famously used by Bitcoin. Here, miners compete to solve puzzles, and the first to crack it gets to add the Block to the blockchain, earning a reward. It's like a race where the winner takes the prize, but it requires a lot of computational power. That is why you hear about massive mining farms filled with specialized hardware.

On the other hand, Proof of Stake (PoS) offers an alternative approach. Instead of racing to solve puzzles, validators are chosen to create new blocks based on the number of coins they hold and are willing to "stake" as collateral. This method is more energy-efficient and doesn't require the same computational effort. Then, there's the option of joining a mining pool, which is like a collaborative effort. Miners pool resources to increase their chances of solving puzzles and then share the rewards among participants. It's teamwork at its finest, making mining more accessible to individuals with less powerful hardware.

Mining hardware has evolved significantly, making it nearly impossible for an average person to mine Bitcoin with a household computer. Today, Bitcoin mining is dominated by industrial-scale operations that use Application-Specific Integrated Circuits (ASICs) —specialized machines designed exclusively for mining. These devices offer the highest efficiency and processing power, far outperforming traditional computers or GPUs. Running a profitable Bitcoin mining operation now requires powerful ASIC hardware, access to low-cost electricity, advanced cooling systems, and participation in large mining pools to compete effectively.

If you're interested in mining other cryptocurrencies, some still allow GPU mining, though even this has become highly competitive. Ethereum, for example, once relied heavily on GPUs, but its shift to proof-of-stake (PoS) with Ethereum 2.0 eliminated mining. Some alternative cryptocurrencies still support GPU mining, but profitability depends on factors like market demand, mining difficulty, and energy costs.

Beyond hardware, mining comes with hidden costs—electricity consumption is a significant factor, as mining rigs require a constant power supply, leading to high energy bills. Additionally, mining generates intense heat, meaning proper cooling systems and ventilation are essential to prevent hardware damage and ensure efficient operation.

For those considering mining, this space has changed significantly from the early days of Bitcoin, where individuals could mine with basic computers. Today, most independent miners join mining pools or invest in cloud mining services rather than setting up their hardware. The key to success is understanding the cost-benefit equation and staying up-to-date with technological advancements in this environment.

All this mining activity doesn't just affect your wallet; it has broader economic implications, too. On a large scale, mining operations can significantly impact energy consumption. Those massive mining farms you hear about consume vast amounts of electricity, sometimes rivaling that of small countries. That has sparked debates about the environmental impact of mining and the need for sustainable practices. However, on a smaller scale, mining can be a source of income for individuals. While it's not the gold rush it once was, savvy miners can still earn a tidy profit if they manage their costs wisely. It's about finding that sweet spot where the rewards outweigh the expenses. For many, it's not just about the money; it's the thrill of being part of a global network, contributing to the creation and validation of digital currency.

With its blend of technology, economics, and community collaboration, mining offers a fascinating glimpse into the world of cryptocurrency. Whether you're considering mining yourself or simply curious about how it all works, understanding these fundamentals gives you a window into the intricate dance that keeps cryptocurrencies alive and thriving.

EXPLORING INITIAL COIN OFFERINGS (ICOS)

Initial Coin Offerings, or ICOs, have become popular for blockchain startups to raise capital. Think of them as crowdfunding for cryptocurrency projects. Instead of seeking traditional venture capital, these projects offer digital tokens to investors, who purchase them using established cryptocurrencies like Bitcoin or Ethereum. In doing so, they bypass traditional financial intermediaries, opening the doors to a global pool of potential investors. This method democratizes fundraising, allowing anyone in the crypto world to invest in the next big thing in the digital finance era.

The ICO process is both fascinating and intricate. It begins with publishing a whitepaper, a detailed document outlining the project's vision, technology, and business plan. This whitepaper is a pitch to potential investors, showcasing why the project is worth their attention and money. Once the whitepaper is released, the project team embarks on a marketing blitz, generating excitement and engaging with the crypto community to attract investment. After generating interest, the next step is the token sale, where investors exchange their cryptocurrency for the project's tokens. The tokens can represent various things, from shares in the project's future profits to utility tokens used within the project's ecosystem. After the sale, these tokens may be distributed to investors and, depending on the project's success, might get listed on cryptocurrency exchanges for public trading.

Investing in ICOs can be a double-edged sword. On one hand, getting in on the ground floor of a promising project can yield substantial returns. Early investors in Ethereum, for instance, saw their investments skyrocket as the platform became a cornerstone of the blockchain ecosystem. However, the potential for high rewards comes hand-in-hand with significant risks. The ICO space is rife with scams and failed projects, making due diligence a crucial step for any investor. It's essential to thoroughly vet the project team, scrutinize the whitepaper, and understand the token's intended use and the market problem it aims to solve. Even then, the lack of regulation in the ICO space means investors have little recourse if a project fails or turns out to be fraudulent.

To illustrate the contrasting outcomes of ICOs, consider Ethereum's meteoric rise. Launched in 2014, Ethereum's ICO raised over $18 million, funding the development of its now-famous blockchain platform that supports smart contracts and decentralized applications. Ethereum's success has made it a staple in the crypto market, and early investors who held onto their tokens have reaped massive profits. On the flip side, there's the infamous BitConnect ICO, a cautionary tale of what can go wrong. Marketed as a high-yield investment program, BitConnect promised investors unrealistic returns through its lending platform. Eventually, it was exposed as a Ponzi scheme, leading to its collapse in 2018 and significant losses for its investors.

Understanding the world of ICOs requires a keen eye and a healthy dose of skepticism. While the allure of discovering the next Ethereum is tempting, it's crucial to approach each opportunity with caution and a critical mindset. By understanding the process and the risks involved, you can better protect yourself against potential pitfalls while exploring the exciting opportunities that ICOs present.

THE RISE OF NON-FUNGIBLE TOKENS (NFTS)

Non-fungible tokens, or NFTs, are essentially digital certificates of ownership stored on a blockchain, a secure and transparent digital ledger. Unlike traditional cryptocurrencies like Bitcoin or Ethereum, which are fungible (meaning one coin is the same as another), NFTs are unique. Each NFT has its specific information and value, making it one-of-a-kind.

NFT is like a digital proof of authenticity for a wide range of digital items—art, music, videos, in-game assets, or even virtual real estate. When you purchase an NFT, you're not necessarily buying the digital file itself but rather the ownership rights to a specific digital asset version.

The magic of NFTs lies in the blockchain technology. The blockchain records every transaction and transfer of ownership, creating a public, tamper-proof history of who owns the NFT. This transparency boosts trust and helps creators receive royalties automatically when their work is resold, thanks to smart contracts embedded in the blockchain.

What makes NFTs even more distinct is that they cannot be split into smaller units. You can't buy half an NFT, which contrasts with cryptocurrencies, where you can purchase fractions of a coin. This indivisibility contributes to their exclusivity and value, particularly in markets driven by collectibility and rarity. Overall, NFTs represent a new way for artists and creators to monetize digital content and for collectors and enthusiasts to purchase and transact digital assets with a transparent and verifiable chain of ownership.

The potential applications for NFTs are as varied as they are exciting. Digital art is probably what you've heard about the most. Artists can sell their work on platforms like OpenSea, where buyers can browse and purchase unique pieces. It's a new frontier for artists, allowing them to reach global audiences without needing galleries or auction houses.

But art isn't the only industry experiencing transformation. Gaming assets are another huge area where NFTs are making waves. In games like Axie Infinity, players can buy, sell, and trade in-game items or characters, each represented as an NFT. This enhances the sense of ownership over digital assets while also creating real-world value for things that were once pixels on a screen. It's like owning a sword or a character in a game that you can sell or trade, just like you would with physical collectibles. It's an exciting blend of digital and tangible worlds, expanding what we consider "ownership."

The impact of NFTs on culture and the economy is profound. For artists and creators, NFTs open up a world of possibilities, empowering them to take control of their work and revenue streams. They are no longer bound by traditional distribution channels; they can sell directly to fans and collectors, keeping a larger share of the profits. This shift democratizes the creative industry, allowing more voices to be heard and more diverse art to be appreciated.

On the flip side, the NFT market is not without its pitfalls. Speculation runs rampant, with prices for some NFTs reaching astronomical heights based solely on hype. This volatility can make the market feel more like a casino than a stable investment platform. While some people have made fortunes, others have seen their investments shrink overnight. It's a dynamic space, constantly changing and evolving, with risks that mirror its potential.

Venturing into the NFT space requires a bit of savvy and a healthy dose of caution. First, assess the value and authenticity of any NFT you're interested in. Just as you'd research a physical artwork before buying, you'll want to ensure the NFT is genuine and worth the investment. Look into the creator's background, the platform's reputation, and any historical sales data available. Also, be aware of the costs involved, particularly gas fees on the Ethereum network. These fees can add up, especially when the network is congested, affecting the final price of your purchase or sale. It's crucial to factor these into your budget to avoid surprises. Staying informed about NFT trends and innovations is equally important. This space is constantly shifting, with new projects and ideas always emerging. Joining online communities, following industry news, and participating in forums can keep you in the loop, helping you make informed decisions.

In the world of NFTs, the possibilities seem endless, connecting art, culture, and technology in ways we've never seen before. As you explore these digital assets, remember that while they offer exciting new opportunities, they also come with challenges. Balancing risk with reward is key, just like with any other investment. Keep your eyes open, stay curious, and you might find yourself at the forefront of the next big thing in the digital age.

As we conclude on NFTs, it's clear they are more than just a fad. They're reshaping how we think about ownership and value in the digital world, and who knows where we are headed as these concepts become increasingly familiar among enthusiasts. With this understanding, you're now ready to explore the fascinating intersection of technology and creativity that NFTs represent.

9
BUILDING LONG-TERM SUCCESS IN CRYPTOCURRENCY

In the current crypto world, there's always a bustling conversation around the latest breakthroughs in cryptocurrency. One moment, there's talk of a new coin that could transform the financial system; the next, a blockchain project emerges that promises to revolutionize an entire industry. With so much happening at once, it's easy to feel overwhelmed. But this rapid pace of change is precisely what makes cryptocurrency so dynamic and full of potential. Thriving in this evolving space requires continuous learning and adaptation. The crypto market is in a constant state of transformation, driven by new technologies, shifting trends, and regulatory developments. Every day brings fresh insights—whether it's an innovative project making waves or a policy shift that could reshape the landscape.

Your ability to learn and adapt is your greatest asset in this fast-paced world. The emergence of new technologies and coins is constant. Today's hot investment could be tomorrow's old news, and you'll want to be ahead of the curve. Staying updated with these changes is crucial to keep your investments relevant and seize opportunities as they arise. Evolving regulatory frameworks add another layer of complexity. Rules and regulations can vary widely by region and shift rapidly, impacting how you invest. Understanding these changes helps you navigate the market safely and ethically, ensuring that your investments are compliant and well-positioned for success.

Regular engagement with educational resources is key to keeping up with the ever-changing crypto landscape. Subscribing to cryptocurrency newsletters is a great way to stay informed. For example, CoinDesk offers a variety of newsletters tailored to different aspects of the crypto world. Whether you're interested in market analysis with the Crypto Daybook Americas or want to explore the technology behind crypto with 'The Protocol', there's something for everyone. These newsletters deliver insights and updates to your inbox, keeping you in the loop without sifting through endless news feeds.

Online courses and webinars are another fantastic resource. They offer structured learning experiences that can deepen your understanding of topics, from blockchain fundamentals to advanced trading strategies. Many of these courses are designed for beginners, providing a solid foundation to build on as you gain more experience. Webinars, often hosted by industry experts, offer the chance to learn about the latest trends and innovations directly from those shaping the crypto world. Participating in these educational opportunities expands your knowledge and connects you with a community of like-minded individuals eager to learn and grow.

Networking with industry experts is equally essential. By attending cryptocurrency conferences, you can immerse yourself in the latest developments and meet professionals at the forefront of the industry. Events like the Crypto Gathering or Consensus Hong Kong provide platforms to learn about emerging trends, discuss challenges, and explore new ideas with peers and leaders in the field. These conferences are not just about listening to presentations; they offer invaluable opportunities for networking and professional development. Engaging with professional crypto networks can also open doors to mentorship and collaboration, providing you with access to insights and expertise that can shape your investment strategy.

Adaptability is the cornerstone of a successful investment strategy in the crypto market. The ability to adjust your portfolio allocations based on new information is crucial. As new technologies emerge or market conditions change, flexibility allows you to pivot and take advantage of new opportunities. For example, if a promising new coin enters the market, allocate a portion of your portfolio while keeping your overall strategy aligned with your long-term goals. Incorporating emerging technologies into your investment plan can also yield significant benefits. Staying open to innovation ensures that your investment portfolio remains dynamic and well-positioned to capitalize on the latest advancements.

Learning and Adaptation Checklist:

- Are you subscribed to informative newsletters to stay updated on market trends?
- Have you enrolled in any online courses or webinars to enhance your understanding of cryptocurrency?
- Are you actively networking with industry experts through conferences or professional networks?
- Do you regularly review and adjust your portfolio to incorporate new information and technologies?

This checklist reminds you of the steps to ensure continuous learning and adaptability in the ever-evolving crypto market. By embracing these practices, you'll be better equipped to steer through the complexities of cryptocurrency investing and build long-term success.

SETTING UP ALERTS AND USING TOOLS FOR BETTER DECISION-MAKING

Your phone buzzes while you're enjoying your morning coffee. A notification flashes across the screen - Bitcoin has jumped 5% in the last hour. In the volatile world of crypto trading, timely information can mean the difference between seizing or missing key opportunities. That's why traders rely on specialized alerts to track market movements. These alerts work like a vigilant market watcher, monitoring price action 24/7. When a cryptocurrency reaches your target price point, you get an instant notification, enabling quick decisions about buying or selling. Beyond just price tracking, you can also set up alerts for major news and regulatory announcements that could affect market direction. This real-time intelligence helps you spot emerging opportunities early and avoid potential market downturns.

Modern trading platforms simplify creating customized market alerts with just a few clicks. Take CoinGecko, for instance. This platform offers a user-friendly interface to set up price alerts for your favorite cryptocurrencies. Start by downloading the CoinGecko mobile app, which is available on iOS and Android. Once installed, sign up or log in to your CoinGecko account to enable the alert functionality. Next, choose the cryptocurrency you want to track from the extensive list. With over 14,000 coins supported, you can customize alerts to suit your portfolio. Click the bell icon next to your chosen coin and set your target price. You can opt for one-time alerts or recurring notifications based on your preferences. This real-time information empowers you to act promptly, ensuring you never miss an opportunity due to market fluctuations.

Beyond price alerts, staying updated with crypto news is equally crucial. Google Alerts can be a game-changer in this regard. To set one up, visit the Google Alerts website and enter the keywords or topics you're interested in, such as "cryptocurrency news" or "Bitcoin regulation." Customize the alert frequency and sources to match your needs, and voilà, you'll receive timely updates directly to your inbox. These alerts will save you time from scouring multiple websites and ensure you remain informed about the latest developments that could impact your investments. Combining price and news alerts, you create a comprehensive system to monitor the crypto market, keeping you ahead of the curve.

In addition to alerts, leveraging tools for enhanced market analysis can significantly improve your decision-making. TradingView is a popular platform offering a robust chart analysis tool suite. It provides detailed graphs and indicators to help you analyze price trends and market behavior. Whether you're a seasoned trader or a beginner, TradingView's intuitive interface makes identifying potential entry and exit points easy, enabling informed decisions.

Sentiment analysis tools are another valuable resource. They aggregate data from social media, news articles, and forums to gauge market sentiment. Understanding the mood and opinions of other investors can offer insights into potential market movements. By utilizing these tools, you gain a deeper understanding of market dynamics, allowing you to make strategic decisions that align with your investment goals.

In the crypto world, timely decision-making can be a game-changer. Alerts and analysis tools equip you with the information to react swiftly to sudden market changes. This agility allows you to capitalize on favorable conditions, whether entering a low-priced market or exiting before a market downturn. By setting up alerts and using analytical tools, you position yourself to make informed decisions, reducing the risk of missed opportunities or ill-timed trades. Remember, in a market as volatile as cryptocurrency, staying informed and ready to act is key to handling the ups and downs with confidence.

STRATEGIZING FOR LONG-TERM GROWTH IN YOUR PORTFOLIO

When building a robust crypto portfolio, the focus often shifts to long-term growth strategies. These strategies revolve around creating a sustainable plan to maneuver through the market's ups and downs while steadily increasing value over time. At the heart of this approach is investing in foundational cryptocurrencies. These are the giants of the crypto world, like Bitcoin and Ethereum, which have established themselves as reliable assets with significant market influence. By allocating a portion of your portfolio to these tried-and-true coins, you lay a solid foundation to support and stabilize your investment strategy.

Another key strategy for long-term success is reinvesting profits to harness the power of compounding. This means taking the gains from your crypto investments and reallocating them into your portfolio, allowing your assets to grow exponentially over time. As your holdings increase, their returns begin accumulating on top of previous gains, creating a snowball effect that accelerates wealth creation. This approach demands patience and discipline, as short-term market swings can be tempting to react to. However, those who commit to reinvesting strategically often see significant growth in their portfolios over the long run. Like building a strong decentralized network, the longer you maintain and expand your investments, the greater the potential rewards.

Balancing your portfolio through regular rebalancing and diversification is another key aspect of long-term success in crypto investments. Rebalancing involves adjusting your portfolio periodically to align with your desired risk level and investment goals. As the value of assets fluctuates, some may become overrepresented in your portfolio, increasing your risk exposure. By rebalancing, you can sell off a portion of these assets and reinvest in others that are underrepresented, maintaining a balanced and diversified portfolio. Diversification is about spreading your investments across a mix of high-risk and stablecoins, reducing the impact of a downturn in any single asset. This approach helps mitigate the risk and positions your portfolio to take advantage of different market opportunities.

Setting milestones and conducting regular reviews are essential for tracking progress and adjusting strategies. Establishing specific milestones, such as achieving a particular portfolio value or reaching a target return on investment, provides clear goals to strive for. Regular reviews, such as quarterly portfolio assessments, allow you to evaluate your performance against these milestones and make informed decisions about any necessary adjustments. Setting performance benchmarks helps you measure success and identify areas for improvement, ensuring that your investment strategy remains on track and aligned with your long-term objectives.

Consider the case of an early Bitcoin adopter who experienced significant growth through a long-term investment strategy. This individual recognized the potential of Bitcoin when it was still in its infancy and decided to hold onto their investment despite market fluctuations. Over the years, as Bitcoin's value increased, so did his portfolio. He achieved substantial returns that far exceeded their initial investment by remaining committed to their long-term strategy and resisting the urge to sell during temporary downturns. This success story illustrates the power of patience and discipline in long-term crypto investing.

Another inspiring example is the story of an investor with a diversified portfolio that consistently yielded positive returns over time. This individual strategically allocated their investments across a variety of cryptocurrencies, including both established coins and promising altcoins. By diversifying their holdings and regularly rebalancing their portfolio, they minimized risk while capitalizing on the growth potential of emerging assets. Their approach allowed them to weather market volatility and achieve steady portfolio growth, highlighting the importance of diversification and strategic asset allocation in long-term success.

However, it's essential to acknowledge the inherent risks of crypto investing. While some investors have seen life-changing gains, others have faced significant losses due to extreme market volatility, regulatory crackdowns, or unforeseen technological flaws. Prices can swing dramatically in short periods, and even promising projects can collapse due to market sentiment, security breaches, or poor execution. Diversification and patience can help mitigate risks, but no strategy guarantees success in an unpredictable environment. Understanding these risks and being prepared for market downturns is just as crucial as chasing potential gains—because opportunities and pitfalls often go hand in hand in the crypto world.

In crypto investing, long-term growth requires a thoughtful and disciplined approach. By focusing on foundational cryptocurrencies, reinvesting returns, rebalancing, and diversifying your portfolio, you can create a strategy that withstands the test of time. Setting milestones and conducting regular reviews provide a framework for tracking progress and making informed decisions. And as demonstrated by successful investors, patience and commitment to a long-term strategy can lead to remarkable results in the ever-evolving crypto market.

LEARNING FROM SUCCESSFUL CRYPTO INVESTORS

In the whirlwind of cryptocurrency investing, looking to those who've already navigated these choppy waters can be invaluable. Studying successful investors is like getting a sneak peek into the strategies and philosophies that have stood the test of time. These individuals have often faced the same uncertainty and made many of the same mistakes you might be wary of now. By analyzing their approaches, you can glean insights that might help you avoid common pitfalls and adopt strategies that align with your goals.

Consider their investment philosophies: some might emphasize the importance of holding tight to your assets through market dips, while others may champion diversification or the exploration of emerging technologies. These differing viewpoints provide a rich tapestry of wisdom from which to draw.

Successful crypto investors typically share a few key traits and habits that set them apart. Discipline is one of the most critical. Sticking to an investment plan despite the market's ups and downs can be challenging, but this steadfastness often distinguishes successful investors. They avoid knee-jerk reactions and understand the value of patience, allowing their investments to grow. Additionally, a willingness to embrace new opportunities and innovations is a hallmark of a savvy investor. The crypto world evolves rapidly, with new coins and technologies emerging regularly. Being open to these changes while doing thorough research can lead to discovering lucrative opportunities others might overlook. Combining discipline with an adaptive mindset allows these investors to capitalize on stability and innovation.

Real-world examples of successful crypto investors offer practical lessons that can inspire and inform your strategies. Take the story of a Bitcoin billionaire who saw the potential of cryptocurrency early on. This investor didn't just stumble upon success; they conducted extensive research, understood the risks, and made calculated decisions. Their journey underscores the importance of foresight and conviction in an investment decision. Alternatively, consider insights from a crypto hedge fund manager who deals with market complexities daily. Through interviews, they often emphasize the significance of data analysis and risk management, highlighting how these tools can guide informed decisions and mitigate potential losses. These stories inspire and demonstrate the diverse paths to success in the crypto market.

No discussion about successful investors is complete without addressing the lessons learned from triumphs and failures. While success stories are uplifting, there's much to learn from the missteps others have endured. Early investors, for instance, sometimes face pitfalls such as investing based on hype without understanding the underlying technology or market dynamics. By studying these experiences, you can better recognize red flags and avoid similar traps. Additionally, examining how investors adapted their strategies during past market cycles can offer guidance on dealing with future fluctuations. Flexibility and learning from history can prepare you for the inevitable ups and downs, allowing you to adjust your approach as needed.

The insights gleaned from successful investors are not just theoretical musings but actionable strategies you can incorporate into your investment practices. Whether it's fostering discipline, remaining open to innovation, or learning from past experiences, these lessons can provide a roadmap for your journey through the dynamic realm of cryptocurrency investing. With each step you take, you'll find yourself better equipped to make informed decisions, seizing opportunities while managing risks with newfound confidence.

Reflection on Success and Failure

- Have you identified any investment philosophies from successful investors that resonate with you?
- Do you practice discipline in sticking to your investment plans, even during market volatility?
- Are you open to exploring new opportunities and innovations in the crypto market?
- Have you learned from the successes and failures of others to refine your investment strategy?

This reflection is a reminder of the importance of adopting key traits from successful investors and learning from their good and bad experiences. As you develop your investment approach, these insights can guide you toward building a more resilient and adaptable portfolio.

In wrapping up this chapter, we've delved into the wisdom of seasoned investors, explored their strategies, and contemplated the lessons they offer. These insights pave the way for continued growth and success in cryptocurrency endeavors. As you move forward, remember that learning from others is just the beginning. Next, we'll explore how to integrate cryptocurrency into your daily life, making it a seamless part of your financial reality.

10

INTEGRATING CRYPTOCURRENCY INTO DAILY LIFE

Envision a future where your digital wallet holds more than just credit cards—it's stocked with cryptocurrencies that you can use for everyday purchases. This shift is no longer hypothetical; it's becoming a reality as digital assets gain mainstream acceptance.

Beyond just investing, cryptocurrencies are reshaping how we handle transactions in daily life. For example, using crypto for online shopping is becoming increasingly common, with more retailers accepting digital currencies for everything from sneakers to tech gadgets. Crypto-based gift cards make spending Bitcoin, Ethereum, or Litecoin at popular stores easier, bridging the gap between digital assets and real-world purchases.

The travel industry is also on board, with airlines and hotels accepting Bitcoin for bookings. Imagine jet-setting to a tropical paradise without ever dealing with currency conversion hassles. Companies like CheapAir make this possible by letting you pay with crypto for flights and accommodation.

The food and beverage sector is also integrating crypto payments. Major restaurant chains and delivery platforms are beginning to accept digital currencies, allowing customers to order meals with Bitcoin or stablecoins. In cities with high crypto adoption, even local coffee shops and food trucks are embracing blockchain payments.

Additionally, the gig economy and freelance platforms are seeing a surge in crypto-based payments. Websites like Bitwage and LaborX enable workers to receive salaries and freelance payments in crypto, offering faster transactions and bypassing traditional banking delays and fees.

Real estate, too, is seeing a blockchain revolution. You can now buy property using Bitcoin, streamlining transactions and cutting out red tape. But beyond just payments, blockchain technology is transforming how contracts are handled through smart contracts—self-executing agreements that automatically enforce the terms once conditions are met. These digital contracts eliminate the need for intermediaries like banks and escrow services, reducing costs and speeding up the buying process. Additionally, because all records are securely stored on the blockchain, ownership transfers are transparent, tamper-proof, and easily verifiable, minimizing fraud and disputes. These developments in the travel and real estate industries show how crypto is breaking down traditional barriers and opening new doors for seamless transactions in various sectors.

Cryptocurrencies are also making waves in philanthropy. Imagine donating to your favorite charity with a few taps on your phone. Crypto donations are now easy and transparent. Blockchain technology lets you track your donation from start to finish, ensuring your funds reach the intended destination. This transparency is a game-changer for nonprofits, building trust with donors and making it easier for them to give. Several charities have embraced crypto donations, recognizing the benefits of faster transactions and lower fees than traditional methods. From supporting global causes to local initiatives, crypto is paving the way for a new era of charitable giving.

To make everyday crypto use even more accessible, a range of services and platforms are at your fingertips. Crypto debit cards are one such innovation, allowing you to spend your digital assets just like cash. These cards convert your crypto into local currency at the point of sale, making it possible to use Bitcoin at your favorite coffee shop or grocery store. Mobile apps also facilitate crypto payments, allowing you to easily transact directly from your smartphone. Whether buying a latte or paying for a ride-share, these apps let you integrate crypto seamlessly into your daily routine, bridging the gap between digital assets and real-world transactions.

Reflection Section: Your Crypto Integration Checklist

- As you start building your portfolio, explore using crypto for online purchases.
- Have you considered travel bookings with Bitcoin?
- Check out crypto donation options for your favorite charities.
- Try a crypto debit card or app for everyday transactions.

This checklist encourages you to explore how cryptocurrencies can integrate into your daily life, making transactions more convenient and secure.

CRYPTOCURRENCY AND E-COMMERCE: A NEW FRONTIER

Checking out at your favorite online store and getting an option to pay with cryptocurrency will soon be a reality. That's right; there will be no more fumbling for your credit card or worrying about currency conversions if you're shopping internationally. More and more online retailers are jumping on the crypto bandwagon, offering digital currencies as a payment option.

Major retailers like Overstock.com have been accepting Bitcoin for years, proving that cryptocurrency payments are more than just a passing trend. With the help of crypto payment gateways like BitPay, businesses can seamlessly integrate digital payments into their systems, making transactions easier for merchants and customers. This shift isn't just appealing to tech-savvy shoppers—it also attracts those who value the security and privacy that cryptocurrencies offer. More importantly, it signals the growing acceptance of digital currency in the mainstream financial reality.

For consumers, using crypto for e-commerce transactions brings several perks. First off, there's the benefit of lower transaction fees. Cryptocurrency transactions are more cost-effective than traditional payment methods that often come with hefty charges. This particularly appeals to cross-border purchases, where currency conversion and international fees usually add up. Additionally, crypto offers faster payments, meaning you can get your products or services without the usual delay caused by bank processing times. Security is another big win—cryptocurrencies use advanced encryption techniques to protect your data, reducing the risk of fraud or identity theft. For merchants, this means fewer chargebacks and disputes, which can be a headache in the e-commerce world.

Shopify, another big name in the e-commerce space, allows its merchants to accept crypto payments, giving them access to a broader audience. This flexibility is crucial in a competitive market, where standing out is key. By accepting Bitcoin and other cryptocurrencies, these platforms not only cater to a growing demand but also position themselves as forward-thinking and innovative. It's a win-win situation where both buyers and sellers benefit. As more platforms adopt these payment methods, we could see a shift where crypto becomes a standard option at checkout, much like PayPal or Apple Pay today.

Crypto technology is fundamentally transforming online shopping. Direct peer-to-peer marketplaces eliminate middlemen, cutting fees while building trust between buyers and sellers. Blockchain-based tracking lets shoppers verify product origins and authenticity instantly. This combination of secure payments and transparent supply chains indicates a future where e-commerce becomes more efficient and trustworthy. For businesses and consumers alike, crypto integration offers new ways to buy, sell, and trade confidently.

USING CRYPTO FOR INTERNATIONAL TRANSACTIONS

Crypto has transformed international payments by solving key problems with traditional money transfers. While banks and wire services charge steep fees for sending funds abroad, cryptocurrency moves value across borders at a fraction of the cost. The decentralized nature of crypto eliminates intermediaries and their associated fees. Sending digital assets directly between parties also avoids currency conversion charges that typically reduce the amount received. This streamlined approach makes international transfers faster and more cost-effective.

Using cryptocurrency for remittances is a fast and cost-effective alternative to traditional money transfer methods. The process is simple: the sender transfers digital currency directly to the recipient's wallet using a crypto wallet. Once received, the recipient can keep or convert the crypto into their local currency through an exchange or crypto-friendly financial service. This method offers several advantages over traditional remittances. Blockchain transactions are often completed in minutes, compared to the days it can take for banks or money transfer services to process international payments. Additionally, crypto remittances bypass intermediaries, reducing transaction fees and increasing financial control for both sender and recipient.

Real-world examples demonstrate how cryptocurrency is transforming global remittances. AZA Finance (formerly BitPesa) provides business-to-business (B2B) financial solutions across Africa. By leveraging blockchain technology, AZA Finance offers faster and more cost-effective cross-border transactions, helping businesses deal with foreign exchange and payments more efficiently. Meanwhile, Ripple has partnered with financial institutions worldwide to streamline international payments. Its blockchain-based RippleNet enables near-instant settlement of cross-border transactions, significantly reducing costs and processing times compared to traditional banking systems.

These innovations highlight the growing impact of blockchain on the financial sector, paving the way for a future where cross-border transactions are seamless, efficient, and more accessible than ever.

Of course, there are challenges to consider. Regulatory hurdles can pose obstacles as governments grapple with categorizing and controlling cryptocurrencies. This uncertainty can make it difficult to make sense of the legal landscape, especially when rules vary from one country to another. Moreover, adoption barriers exist in recipient countries where infrastructure for crypto transactions may be lacking. To create a more inclusive system, overcoming these challenges requires collaboration between governments, tech companies, and financial institutions. With ongoing efforts to educate users and develop supportive regulations, the potential for crypto to transform international transactions remains promising, paving the way for a more connected world.

THE ROLE OF CRYPTO IN PERSONAL FINANCIAL PLANNING

Integrating cryptocurrency into your financial strategy can enhance your overall portfolio strength. Adding digital assets to traditional investments creates new opportunities for growth while potentially protecting against inflation. Conventional currencies are subject to central bank monetary policies, which can increase money supply and potentially decrease purchasing power over time. Cryptocurrencies, however, have built-in scarcity that can help preserve purchasing power, like Bitcoin. This makes crypto assets a strategic addition for investors focused on long-term value preservation and portfolio diversification.

Managing crypto finances effectively requires the right tools to stay organized and informed. There are specialized apps designed for crypto portfolio management, some of which are mentioned throughout this book, that make tracking your investments simple. These apps provide real-time data, performance monitoring, and alerts for price fluctuations, helping you stay on top of market movements.

Additionally, budgeting tools that integrate crypto assets allow you to see how your digital holdings fit into your financial picture, making it easier to plan and make informed decisions. By using the right resources, managing your digital assets becomes more efficient and less overwhelming, ensuring you control your financial strategy.

Of course, including crypto in your financial plan comes with benefits and risks, just like any investment. On the upside, the potential for high returns is a significant draw. Cryptocurrencies are known to appreciate dramatically, offering substantial gains if timed correctly. However, the flip side is market volatility. Prices can swing wildly, and what goes up can come down just as fast. It's this rollercoaster nature that requires careful consideration and risk management. You should weigh these factors carefully, like checking the weather before a road trip, to ensure you're prepared for whatever the market throws.

To approach cryptocurrency investing responsibly, setting clear financial goals is key. Whether you're looking to save for a big purchase or plan for retirement, having specific targets in mind can guide your investment strategy. Regularly reviewing and adjusting your allocations is also important. The crypto market is dynamic, and what works today might not be as effective tomorrow. By staying flexible and open to change, you can adapt to market shifts and keep your financial plan on track. It's like adjusting your sails to catch the wind, ensuring you're always moving in the right direction.

FINDING BALANCE: INTEGRATING CRYPTO WITH TRADITIONAL INVESTMENTS

Think of your investment portfolio as a well-structured plan where each asset plays a role in building long-term financial stability. Integrating cryptocurrency alongside traditional investments like stocks and bonds introduces diversification, helping you to manage risk while expanding growth opportunities. A balanced portfolio involves distributing investments across different asset classes, ensuring resilience in varying market conditions. Incorporating traditional and digital assets creates a dynamic financial strategy that embraces innovation while maintaining stability.

Determining the right crypto allocation in your portfolio is crucial. It's not about throwing all your savings into Bitcoin or Ethereum overnight but finding a good balance that aligns with your risk tolerance and financial goals. Start by assessing how much risk you're comfortable with. Cryptocurrencies can be volatile, so a smaller allocation might suit more conservative investors, while those with a higher risk appetite might allocate more. Regularly rebalancing your portfolio is key. Market conditions change, and what was a reasonable allocation last year might not suit the current reality. Periodic reviews help you adjust your investments, ensuring they align with your objectives.

Diversification is a key concept for a reason — it's a smart way to reduce risk. Including crypto in your portfolio can enhance diversification, offering exposure to emerging technologies and trends that traditional assets might miss. Think of it as adding a new flavor to your investment mix that can potentially offset the ups and downs of other markets. Crypto's unique characteristics, like its decentralized nature, provide a hedge against economic uncertainties affecting conventional markets. This exposure to new sectors can be a game-changer, especially as blockchain technology continues to evolve and influence various industries.

Real-world examples illustrate how investors successfully integrate crypto into their portfolios. Consider how a crypto hedge fund can achieve balance by allocating a portion to established cryptocurrencies while maintaining investments in traditional assets. This approach allows them to capitalize on crypto's growth while minimizing risk through diversification. On a more personal level, you could diversify your portfolio by adding a modest crypto allocation. They don't need to go all-in but strategically include digital assets to complement your stocks and bonds. Over time, this balance provides stability and growth, showing that integrating crypto with traditional investments doesn't require a complete overhaul. Instead, it's about adding a new dimension to your financial strategy that adapts to the ever-changing investment landscape.

STAYING UPDATED: RELIABLE SOURCES FOR CRYPTO NEWS

In the fast-paced world of cryptocurrency, staying informed is crucial. Market conditions can change at a rapid pace, driven by technological innovations and shifting investor sentiment. The dynamic nature of the crypto market means that being well-informed is not just recommended—it's essential for making smart investment decisions. If you're not keeping up, you might be caught off guard by sudden price swings or new developments that could impact your portfolio. We have touched on some of these resources throughout this book, but here's a quick recap for your reference.

You need reliable sources that provide accurate and timely information to stay ahead. CoinDesk is a great place to start, offering comprehensive industry updates and insights. It's like having a finger on the pulse of the crypto world, delivering news on everything from market trends to regulatory shifts. The Block is another trusted source for deeper analysis, diving into the complexities of the crypto market with detailed reports and expert opinions. CoinMarketCap is essential for tracking real-time cryptocurrency prices, market capitalizations, and trends, helping traders make informed decisions. TradingView, on the other hand, provides powerful charting tools and technical analysis, making it a go-to platform for traders looking to analyze price movements and market patterns.

These platforms are invaluable for staying informed, offering a wealth of information and analysis that helps you make informed decisions. They cover a wide range of topics, allowing you to explore different aspects of the crypto market, from real-time price tracking and technical analysis to in-depth reports on regulations, innovations, and emerging trends. Whether you're a trader analyzing price movements on TradingView, an investor tracking market caps on CoinMarketCap, or a researcher diving into expert insights from

CoinDesk and The Block, these resources provide the essential data and perspectives needed to explore the fast-paced world of crypto.

Social media and community forums are also rich sources of information. Platforms like Crypto Twitter allow you to engage with industry experts and enthusiasts, providing real-time discussions and insights. It's a lively space to catch up on the latest news, hear diverse perspectives, and join conversations about emerging trends. Reddit, with its numerous crypto-focused subreddits, is another hub for staying updated. These forums are filled with discussions and debates, offering a grassroots perspective on what's happening in the crypto world. Engaging with these communities keeps you informed and connects you with others who share your interests.

However, not all sources are created equal, so it's essential to evaluate the credibility of the information you consume. Start by checking the author's credentials to ensure they have a background that supports their claims. Look for signs of expertise or affiliation with reputable institutions. Verifying information through multiple sources is also key. Cross-referencing news articles or reports can help confirm their accuracy, reducing the risk of misinformation. This practice is crucial, especially in volatile and sometimes speculative spaces like cryptocurrency. By discerning your sources, you can confidently conquer the crypto space, armed with reliable information that guides your investment choices.

THE FUTURE OF CRYPTOCURRENCY: PREPARING FOR WHAT'S NEXT

The crypto realm is constantly shifting, with new trends and innovations always emerging. One of the most exciting areas to watch is advancements in blockchain technology. Developers continually find ways to make blockchains more efficient and scalable, solving the pesky issue of slow transaction speeds that plagued earlier systems. These improvements could open the door for even greater adoption as faster and more secure networks become the norm. New use cases are also cropping up, extending beyond the financial sector. Think about decentralized identity management or supply chain transparency—these are just a couple of examples of how blockchain could revolutionize industries we interact with daily. The possibilities seem endless, and watching these developments could offer you a front-row seat to witnessing groundbreaking changes.

Regulation is another key factor that will shape the future of cryptocurrencies. As governments worldwide grapple with classifying and controlling digital assets, the rules are bound to change. Future regulations could lead to increased institutional adoption, as more explicit rules make large financial players more comfortable entering the market. This could bring a new wave of credibility and stability to the crypto space. Enhanced consumer protection measures are also likely to emerge, providing peace of mind for investors worried about security and fraud. While regulations might seem like a burden, they can foster a healthier market environment by weeding out bad actors and encouraging legitimate growth.

Flexibility and adaptability will be your greatest allies as the crypto landscape evolves. Staying open to new technologies means you can seize opportunities as they arise. Whether it's a groundbreaking new blockchain platform or an innovative crypto application, being willing to explore and learn will keep you ahead of the curve. Regularly reevaluating your investment strategies is also crucial. What worked last year might not be the best approach today, so staying flexible allows you to adjust your sails and steer your investments in the right direction. Embracing change with an open mind can position you to capitalize on the dynamic nature of the crypto world.

To secure the long-term success of your crypto investments, focus on projects with strong fundamentals and real-world applications. Investing in well-established blockchain technologies provides a solid foundation and reduces exposure to high-risk, speculative assets. Diversifying across different blockchain platforms is another smart strategy. Spreading investments across different projects minimizes risk if one technology encounters setbacks while also increasing the potential to capitalize on emerging innovations. Maintaining a balanced and forward-looking portfolio can mitigate risks and position yourself for long-term growth in the ever-evolving cryptocurrency market.

KEEPING THE CRYPTO JOURNEY ALIVE

Now that you have everything you need to start investing in cryptocurrency with confidence, it's time to pay it forward!

By sharing your honest review on Amazon, you'll help other beginners—just like you once were—find the right guidance to navigate the world of crypto safely and smartly.

Your review could be the reason someone takes their first step toward financial independence, avoids costly mistakes, or finally understands how crypto really works.

Thank you for your support. Cryptocurrency education stays alive when we share what we've learned—and you're helping me do just that.

Simply scan the QR code below or click this link to leave a review:

With gratitude,
Pinnacle Insights

CONCLUSION

Wow, what a journey it's been! We've covered so much ground together in this book, from the basics of cryptocurrency to advanced strategies for long-term success. I hope you're feeling more confident and excited about the incredible opportunities that await you in the world of crypto investing.

Let's take a moment to reflect on the key takeaways. First and foremost, you've learned that cryptocurrency is more than just a trend—it's a revolutionary technology with the potential to transform the way we think about money and value. By understanding the fundamentals of blockchain, you've gained a solid foundation for exploring this exciting new reality.

But knowledge alone isn't enough. To succeed as a crypto investor, you need a strategic approach that balances risk and return. That's why we've explored various investment strategies, from long-term holding to diversification and rebalancing. You now have the tools to build a portfolio that aligns with your goals and risk tolerance.

Of course, investing in cryptocurrency isn't without its challenges. From market volatility to security concerns, there are plenty of pitfalls to watch out for. But armed with the insights and best practices shared in this book, you're well-equipped to chart your way through these challenges with confidence.

So, what's next? The journey doesn't end here. In fact, it's just beginning. The crypto world is constantly evolving, with new technologies, regulations, and opportunities always emerging. From groundbreaking advancements in decentralized finance (DeFi) to the rapid growth of non-fungible tokens (NFTs) and the expansion of blockchain use cases beyond finance, the scenario is full of innovation. New projects, protocols, and digital assets continue to reshape industries, offering unprecedented possibilities for investors, developers, and enthusiasts alike. Whether it's the rise of Web3, the evolution of smart contracts, or the increasing adoption of crypto in mainstream finance, the space is teeming with potential. It's crucial to keep learning and adapting to stay ahead of the curve—because, in crypto, the next big thing is always just around the corner.

My call to action is simple: take what you've learned and put it into practice. Start small if needed, but don't be afraid to dive in and explore. Join communities, attend events, and surround yourself with like-minded individuals who share your passion for crypto. The more you engage with this exciting world, the more opportunities you'll discover.

Remember, success in crypto investing isn't just about making money. It's about being part of a transformative movement that is reshaping the very foundations of finance and technology. Blockchain and cryptocurrencies are revolutionizing how people transact, store value, and interact with digital assets, fostering a more decentralized and inclusive financial system. This shift is breaking down traditional barriers, giving individuals more control over their wealth, and enabling new economic models previously unimaginable.

By embracing this new frontier, you're not just investing in your financial future—you're supporting innovation that has the potential to empower the unbanked, streamline global commerce, and redefine trust in digital transactions. Every investment, every adoption of blockchain solutions, and every step forward in this space contributes to a broader movement shaping the next era of technology. Your participation in crypto is more than a financial decision—it's a commitment to being part of a global revolution that is still unfolding.

As we come to the end of this book, I want to take a moment to express my gratitude for sharing this journey with me. Exploring the world of cryptocurrency is an exciting and ever-evolving experience. I hope this book has given you valuable insights and the confidence to start exploring it successfully. It has been a privilege to share my knowledge and experiences, and I look forward to seeing how you apply them in your crypto journey.

This space is continuously growing, with new opportunities, challenges, and innovations emerging daily. Staying informed, adapting to changes, and making well-researched decisions will be key to your success. Whether you're investing, building, or simply exploring the potential of blockchain technology, know that the learning never stops.

So, here's to your success as a crypto investor! May you have the courage to take risks, the wisdom to learn from your mistakes, and the vision to see the incredible potential ahead. Together, we can build a future where cryptocurrency is not just a niche investment but a mainstream tool for financial empowerment and innovation.

Keep learning, growing, and, most importantly, believing in yourself.

The future of finance is yours to shape, and I can't wait to see what you'll achieve.

Happy investing!

GLOSSARY OF CRYPTO TERMS

- **Address** - A unique string of characters used to send and receive cryptocurrency transactions.
- **Airdrop** - A distribution of free tokens or coins to promote a cryptocurrency or blockchain project.
- **Altcoin** - Any cryptocurrency other than Bitcoin.
- **Arbitrage** - The practice of buying cryptocurrency on one exchange and selling it on another for profit.
- **ATH (All-Time High)** - The highest price a cryptocurrency has ever reached.
- **Bear Market** - A prolonged period of declining cryptocurrency prices.
- **Block** - A set of transactions that are confirmed and added to a blockchain.
- **Blockchain** - A decentralized, distributed ledger that records all transactions across a network.
- **Block Reward** - The reward given to miners for successfully validating a block of transactions.
- **Bull Market** - A prolonged period of rising cryptocurrency prices.
- **Centralized Exchange (CEX)** - A cryptocurrency exchange managed by a central authority.
- **Cold Wallet** - A cryptocurrency storage method that keeps funds offline for security purposes.
- **Consensus Mechanism** - The method used by blockchain networks to validate transactions, such as Proof of Work (PoW) or Proof of Stake (PoS).
- **Cryptocurrency** - A digital or virtual currency that uses cryptography for security.
- **Cryptography** - The practice of securing information through mathematical techniques.
- **DAO (Decentralized Autonomous Organization)** - A blockchain-based organization that operates without centralized control, using smart contracts.
- **Decentralized Finance (DeFi)** - A financial system built on blockchain that operates without intermediaries like banks.
- **Decentralized Exchange (DEX)** - A peer-to-peer marketplace for trading cryptocurrencies without a central authority.
- **DYOR (Do Your Own Research)** - A common phrase in crypto advising investors to research before making investment decisions.

- **Fiat Currency** - Government-issued currency that is not backed by a physical commodity, such as the U.S. Dollar.
- **Fork** - A change in a blockchain's protocol that creates a new version of the blockchain.
- **FOMO (Fear of Missing Out)** - The feeling of urgency to invest in a cryptocurrency due to its rising price.
- **FUD (Fear, Uncertainty, Doubt)** - Negative information or misinformation that creates panic among investors.
- **Gas Fees** - Transaction fees paid on blockchain networks, especially Ethereum, to compensate for computational effort.
- **Genesis Block** - The first block ever mined in a blockchain network.
- **HODL** - A term derived from "hold," meaning to keep cryptocurrency investments despite market fluctuations.
- **ICO (Initial Coin Offering)** - A fundraising method where new cryptocurrencies are sold to investors before launch.
- **Liquidity** - The ease with which a cryptocurrency can be bought or sold without significantly affecting its price.
- **Market Capitalization (Market Cap)** - The total value of a cryptocurrency, calculated by multiplying its price by the circulating supply.
- **Meme Coin** - A cryptocurrency created as a joke or meme, often experiencing extreme volatility.
- **Mining** - The process of validating blockchain transactions and earning rewards in the form of cryptocurrency.
- **Mooning** - A slang term describing a cryptocurrency experiencing rapid price increases.
- **NFT (Non-Fungible Token)** - A unique digital asset stored on a blockchain, often representing art, collectibles, or music.
- **Node** - A computer that participates in maintaining the blockchain network.
- **Oracle** - A service that provides external data to smart contracts on a blockchain.
- **Paper Hands** - A term referring to investors who sell their assets quickly due to fear of losses.
- **Private Key** - A secure code that grants access to a cryptocurrency wallet.
- **Proof of Stake (PoS)** - A consensus mechanism where validators are chosen based on the amount of cryptocurrency they hold and stake.
- **Proof of Work (PoW)** - A consensus mechanism that requires computational power to validate transactions and mine new blocks.

- **Public Key** - A cryptographic code that allows others to send cryptocurrency to a wallet.
- **Pump and Dump** - A market manipulation scheme where the price of a cryptocurrency is artificially inflated before being sold off.
- **Rug Pull** - A scam where developers abandon a project after collecting investor funds.
- **Satoshi** - The smallest unit of Bitcoin, named after its creator, Satoshi Nakamoto.
- **Seed Phrase** - A series of words used to recover a cryptocurrency wallet.
- **Smart Contract** - A self-executing contract with terms directly written into code.
- **Stablecoin** - A cryptocurrency pegged to the value of a stable asset, like the U.S. dollar, to reduce volatility.
- **Staking** - The process of locking up cryptocurrency to support network operations and earn rewards.
- **Token** - A digital asset issued on a blockchain, often representing ownership, access, or value.
- **Utility Token** - A token that provides access to a specific product or service within a blockchain ecosystem.
- **Volatility** - The measure of how much a cryptocurrency's price fluctuates over time.
- **Whale** - describes an individual or entity that holds a large amount of a particular cryptocurrency. Whales have the potential to influence market prices due to the size of their trades, often causing significant price movements when they buy or sell in large quantities.
- **Wallet** - A digital tool used to store, send, and receive cryptocurrencies.
- **Web3** - A decentralized version of the internet built on blockchain technology, emphasizing user ownership and privacy.

REFERENCES

NerdWallet. (n.d.). *Cryptocurrency basics: Pros, cons and how it works.* Retrieved from https://www.nerdwallet.com/article/investing/cryptocurrency

Investopedia. (n.d.). *Blockchain facts: What is it, how it works, and how it can be used.* Retrieved from https://www.investopedia.com/terms/b/blockchain.asp

Wikipedia contributors. (n.d.). *Satoshi Nakamoto.* Wikipedia, The Free Encyclopedia. Retrieved from https://en.wikipedia.org/wiki/Satoshi_Nakamoto

Built In. (n.d.). *20 popular altcoins to know.* Retrieved from https://builtin.com/blockchain/altcoins

Coin Bureau. (n.d.). *The best beginner-friendly crypto wallets you should try.* Retrieved from https://coinbureau.com/analysis/top-crypto-wallets-for-beginners/

One Trading. (n.d.). *How to choose the best crypto exchange: 10 essential tips.* Retrieved from https://onetrading.com/blogs/10-essential-tips-for-choosing-the-best-crypto-exchange

NerdWallet. (n.d.). *How to buy cryptocurrency: What investors should know.* Retrieved from https://www.nerdwallet.com/article/investing/how-to-buy-cryptocurrency

SwissMoney. (2024). *Crypto transaction fees: A beginner guide.* Retrieved from https://swissmoney.com/cryptocurrency-transaction-fees

ICONOMI. (2024). *Short-term vs. long-term crypto investment strategies.* Retrieved from https://www.iconomi.com/blog/short-term-vs-long-term-crypto-investing

U.S. News & World Report. (n.d.). *8 ways to diversify your crypto portfolio and limit risk.* Retrieved from https://money.usnews.com/investing/cryptocurrency/articles/ways-to-diversify-your-crypto-portfolio-and-limit-risk

StormGain. (n.d.). *Risk management basics for crypto beginners.* Retrieved from https://stormgain.com/blog/risk-management-basics-for-crypto-beginners

Archax. (n.d.). *Crypto market analysis & trends.* Retrieved from https://archax.com/academy/crypto-market-analysis-trends

Internet Crime Complaint Center (IC3). (2023). *Cryptocurrency fraud report 2023.* Retrieved from https://www.ic3.gov/annualreport/reports/2023_ic3cryptocurrencyreport.pdf

Cointelegraph. (n.d.). *What is two-factor authentication (2FA) and how to use it?* Retrieved from https://cointelegraph.com/learn/articles/what-is-two-factor-authentication-2fa

Coin Bureau. (2025). *Compare the top 6 crypto hardware wallets in 2025.* Retrieved from https://coinbureau.com/analysis/best-hardware-wallets/

Genius Yield Academy. (n.d.). *What are crypto phishing attacks and how to prevent them?* Retrieved from https://academy.geniusyield.co/articles/what-are-crypto-phishing-attacks-and-how-to-prevent-them-genius-academy

CryptoPanic. (n.d.). *CryptoPanic - News aggregator platform indicating impact on crypto markets.* Retrieved from https://cryptopanic.com/

CNBC Select. (n.d.). *Invest in cryptocurrency responsibly with these 3 steps.* Retrieved from https://www.cnbc.com/select/steps-to-dip-your-toes-into-crypto-responsibly/

Bamboo. (n.d.). *Crypto glossary: The beginner's guide to crypto-lingo.* Retrieved from https://www.getbamboo.io/blog/Beginners-Guide-To-Crypto/

BitDegree. (n.d.). *Crypto Discords: Connect with fellow crypto enthusiasts.* Retrieved from https://www.bitdegree.org/crypto/tutorials/crypto-discords

Coinbase. (n.d.). *What is a bull or bear market?* Retrieved from https://www.coinbase.-com/learn/crypto-basics/what-is-a-bull-or-bear-market#:~:text=To%20put%20it%20simply%2C%20a,mostly%20up-ward%20or%20downward%20movement

NinjaPromo. (n.d.). *Top 36 crypto tools for analysis, trading & research.* Retrieved from https://ninjapromo.io/best-crypto-tools-for-analysis-trading-research

Yale University. (n.d.). *Exploring the relationship between Bitcoin price and global economic events.* Retrieved from https://campuspress.yale.edu/wave/exploring-the-relationship-between-bitcoin-price-and-global-economic-events/

The Economic Times. (n.d.). *Crypto market insights: Effective strategies for volatile conditions.* Retrieved from https://m.economictimes.com/markets/cryptocurrency/crypto-market-insights-effective-strategies-for-volatile-conditions/articleshow/112564285.cms

U.S. Securities and Exchange Commission (SEC). (n.d.). *Crypto assets.* Retrieved from https://www.sec.gov/securities-topics/crypto-assets

Financial Conduct Authority (FCA). (n.d.). *Guidance for crypto firms to help them comply with marketing rules.* Retrieved from https://www.fca.org.uk/news/news-stories/guidance-crypto-firms-help-them-comply-marketing-rules

Simple. (n.d.). *Crypto ESG investing.* Retrieved from https://simple.app/blog/crypto-esg-investing/

Internal Revenue Service (IRS). (n.d.). *Digital assets.* Retrieved from https://www.irs.-gov/businesses/small-businesses-self-employed/digital-assets

Investopedia. (n.d.). *What is decentralized finance (DeFi) and how does it work?* Retrieved from https://www.investopedia.com/decentralized-finance-defi-5113835

Investopedia. (n.d.). *How does Bitcoin mining work? A beginner's guide.* Retrieved from https://www.investopedia.com/tech/how-does-bitcoin-mining-work/

Vezgo. (n.d.). *Initial coin offerings (ICOs): Risks and rewards.* Retrieved from https://vezgo.com/blog/initial-coin-offering-risk-reward/

Keeper Solutions. (n.d.). *Understanding NFTs and their impact on art, culture, and the environment.* Retrieved from https://keepersolutions.com/understanding-nfts-and-their-impact-on-art-culture-and-the-environment/

CoinDesk. (n.d.). *Newsletters.* Retrieved from https://www.coindesk.com/newsletters

NinjaPromo. (2025). *25 best crypto conferences & events to attend in 2025.* Retrieved from https://ninjapromo.io/best-crypto-conferences

CoinGecko. (n.d.). *How to set up the price alert function on CoinGecko.* Retrieved from https://www.coingecko.com/learn/how-to-set-up-the-price-alert-function-on-coingecko

Quora. (n.d.). *Who are some of the most successful cryptocurrency investors and what advice can they offer for investing in crypto?* Retrieved from https://www.quora.com/Who-are-some-of-the-most-successful-cryptocurrency-investors-and-what-advice-can-they-offer-for-investing-in-crypto

The Block. (n.d.). *What are practical use cases of cryptocurrencies?* Retrieved from https://www.theblock.co/learn/245722/what-are-practical-use-cases-of-cryptocurrencies

Tangem. (2023). *Top companies that accept crypto as payment in 2023.* Retrieved from https://tangem.com/en/blog/post/where-to-pay-in-crypto-an-overview-of-companies-and-services/

Fiat Republic. (n.d.). *How to transfer money to another country with crypto: Disrupting the remittance market.* Retrieved from https://fiatrepublic.com/how-to-transfer-money-to-another-country-with-crypto-disrupting-the-remittance-market/

BYDFi. (n.d.). *What are the best crypto news platforms for beginners?* Retrieved from https://www.bydfi.com/en/questions/what-are-the-best-crypto-news-platforms-for-beginners

www.ingramcontent.com/pod-product-compliance
Lightning Source LLC
LaVergne TN
LVHW022228200926
848481LV00006B/2166